simple, fun & quickly done

18 EASY-TO-SEW TABLE RUNNERS, BAGS, PILLOWS, *and more*

TERRY ATKINSON

Martingale
Create with Confidence

Simple, Fun & Quickly Done:
18 Easy-to-Sew Table Runners, Bags, Pillows, and More
© 2017 by Terry Atkinson

Martingale®
19021 120th Ave. NE, Ste. 102
Bothell, WA 98011-9511 USA
ShopMartingale.com

Printed in China
22 21 20 19 18 17   8 7 6 5 4 3 2 1

Library of Congress Cataloging-in-Publication Data
is available upon request.

ISBN: 978-1-60468-834-4

MISSION STATEMENT

We empower makers who use fabric and yarn
to make life more enjoyable.

CREDITS

PUBLISHER AND
CHIEF VISIONARY OFFICER
Jennifer Erbe Keltner

CONTENT DIRECTOR
Karen Costello Soltys

DESIGN MANAGER
Adrienne Smitke

MANAGING EDITOR
Tina Cook

PRODUCTION MANAGER
Regina Girard

ACQUISITIONS EDITOR
Karen M. Burns

PHOTOGRAPHER
Brent Kane

TECHNICAL EDITOR
Beese Enterprises, Inc.

ILLUSTRATOR
Christine Erikson

COPY EDITOR
Sheila Chapman Ryan

SPECIAL THANKS

*Thanks to Brian Shook and Jodi Davis of
Edmonds, Washington, for allowing the photography
for this book to take place in their home.*

Contents

Introduction 5

PROJECTS

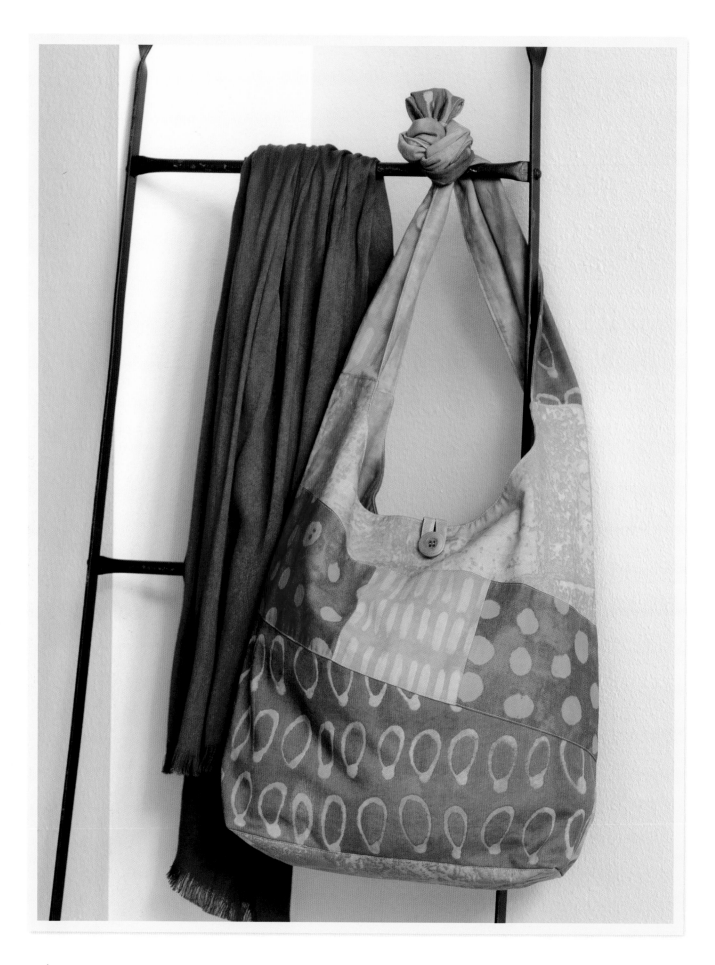

Introduction

Let's have some fun! No one needs a hobby that adds more stress or struggle to life. That's the spirit that guides my thinking as I'm designing simple quilt, pillow, and bag patterns, as well as other miscellany that adds a smile to my face. What you'll find in the pages that follow is a collection of my favorite go-to items, not just for my own home, but for making gifts as well.

I'll share lots of shortcuts, tips, and tricks to make sure you love not only the results but also the process of making these patterns. And, as a former home ec teacher (no kidding! I'm the one you'll wish you'd had!), I've taught plenty of students who started with little or no sewing knowledge. That's how I approach these patterns. You don't have to be a zipper genius (you might even have zipper-phobia)—just follow my fast and fun method for putting one in a pillow or bag. It's easy! I promise!

I think of myself as a modern quilt designer with a traditional piece-maker's heart. Everything here is easy to sew and fun to make ... so let's get sewing!

~Terry

✳ TERRY'S TIP

A Note about Zippers

Many of the projects in this book call for zippers. Make sure you choose ones with nylon or polyester coils instead of metal teeth so that you can stitch over them and trim them to size.

If you aren't able to locate the type of zipper you want, visit my website, AtkinsonDesigns.com, to find an online retailer or nearby shop that carries my coil zippers. They're available in 36 beautiful colors.

Citrus Slices Hot Pad

Add a splash of sunshine to your kitchen with your favorite fruit colors.
These sweet hot pads are made with wedges cut from a simple strip set.

✳ **FINISHED SIZE: 10" × 5⅜"** ✳

MATERIALS

Fat quarters measure 18" × 21". Fat eighths measure 9" × 21". Makes 1 hot pad.

1 fat quarter of light orange batik for hot-pad top and backing

1 fat quarter of dark orange batik for hot-pad top and binding

1 fat eighth of white batik for hot-pad top

6" × 11" rectangle of lightweight cotton batting

¼ yard of 22½"-wide Insul-Bright insulated batting*

Chalk marker or water-soluble marker

Freezer paper for cutting templates

Optional:

✳ 18° Circle Segment Ruler (Creative Grids) for cutting template-free wedges (see page 8)

✳ Wonder Clips (Clover) for securing multiple layers of fabric

✳ Round Up Tool (Creative Grids) for trimming the curved edge

If you're making multiple hot pads, ¼ yard of Insul-Bright is enough to make 2 hot pads; ⅓ yard is enough to make 3.

CUTTING

All strips are cut on the straight grain unless otherwise noted.

From the light orange batik, cut:
1 strip, 4¼" × 21"
1 rectangle, 7" × 11"
Set aside the remainder of the light orange batik for step 5.

From the dark orange batik, cut:
1 strip, 1½" × 21"
1 strip, 1" × 21"
1 strip, 2½" × 18", *on the bias*

From the white batik, cut:
1 strip, 1¼" × 21"
1 strip, 1" × 21"

From the Insul-Bright, cut:
1 rectangle, 6" × 11"

Cutting Wedges: Two Options

In step 3 at right, you'll cut wedges from a strip set. To cut the wedges with a template, trace the pattern on page 10 onto freezer paper three to four times and cut out the templates on the pencil lines. Position the freezer-paper templates shiny side down on the fabric, keeping the wide end even with the edge of the strip set. Press with a dry iron. Cut out each fabric shape along the edge of the paper. Each freezer-paper template can be reused several times until it no longer sticks to the fabric.

If you want to use the 18° Circle Segment Ruler to cut your wedges instead, here's how it works. Align the 4" line on the ruler with the bottom of the strip set. Use a rotary cutter to cut the wedge shape. Then align the 4" line with the top of the strip set to cut a second wedge shape. Repeat to cut 10 wedges.

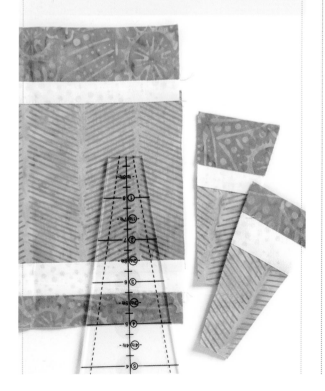

MAKING THE HOT PAD

Use a ¼"-wide seam allowance throughout unless otherwise noted.

1. Sew together the white 1" × 21" strip, the dark orange 1½" × 21" strip, and the light orange 4¼" × 21" strip as shown in step 2. Press the seam allowances away from the light orange strip. The strip set should measure 5¾" × 21".

2. Stitch the white 1¼" × 21" strip and the dark orange 1" × 21" strip to the strip set as shown. Press the seam allowances away from the light orange strip. The strip set should now measure 7" × 21".

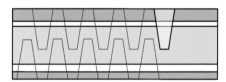

3. Use the wedge pattern on page 10 or an 18° Circle Segment Ruler (see "Cutting Wedges: Two Options" at left) to cut five wedges each from the top and bottom of the strip set (for a total of 10 wedges).

4. Arrange the wedge units in a fan shape, alternating wedges as shown. Pin and stitch the wedges together, being careful not to stretch the edges. Press all the seam allowances in one direction. The bottom edge should make a straight line; if it doesn't, trim with a rotary cutter.

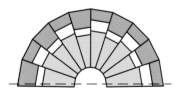

Trim bottom edge straight.

5. Trace the half-circle pattern on page 10 onto freezer paper and cut it out on the drawn lines. Using a dry iron and keeping the shiny side down, press the freezer-paper template to the wrong side of a scrap of the remaining light orange batik. Cut out the shape, adding a ¼" seam allowance along the curved edge. Finger-press the seam allowance around the edge of the paper toward the wrong side as shown. Hand baste. Press.

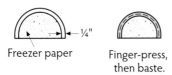

Freezer paper

Finger-press, then baste.

6. Position the half circle at the center of the fan unit as shown, aligning the straight edges. Pin. Using thread to match the half circle, hand appliqué in place with a small slip stitch. Remove the basting stitches and freezer paper. Press.

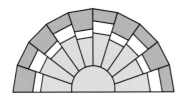

7. Aligning the straight edges, position the batting on top of the Insul-Bright rectangle. Position the fan unit, right side up, on top with the straight edges even. Place the light orange rectangle on top, aligning the bottom edges and keeping right sides together. Pin. Using a walking foot, stitch a ¼" seam along the bottom edge through all layers.

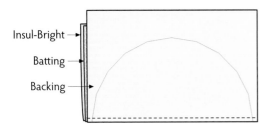

Insul-Bright

Batting

Backing

8. Wrap the light orange rectangle around to the back. You'll see about ⅜" of light orange along the seam. Stitch in the ditch along the seam. It's OK if the raw edges are not even.

✳ **TERRY'S TIP**

Wonder Clips to the Rescue

I like to use Wonder Clips to hold the edges together because it's hard to pin through so many layers.

9. Stitch a scant ¼" from the curved edge, stitching through all layers. Stitch in the ditch along alternating seams as shown. I like to mark the stitching lines within the half circle so that I'm sure where to stitch. **Note:** The hot pad will be too stiff if you stitch along every seam.

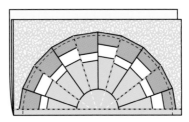

Stitch in the ditch.

FINISHING THE HOT PAD

1. Using scissors or the Round Up Tool (see "Cutting Half Circles with a Ruler" at right), cut the hot pad into a half circle by trimming the excess batting, Insul-Bright, and light orange rectangle even with the top of the hot pad.

2. Press the dark-orange 2½" × 18" bias strip in half lengthwise with wrong sides together. Leaving at least ½" of binding extending beyond the straight edge of the hot pad, stitch the binding to the curved edge of the hot pad. Press the binding strip toward the outer raw edges of the hot pad,

then trim the binding-strip ends ½" from the straight edge of the hot pad. Wrap the ends to the back to cover the raw edge, then fold the binding to the back. Stitch in place by hand or machine.

* **TERRY'S TIP**

Cutting Half Circles with a Ruler

If you prefer rulers to templates, try using a Round Up Tool to trim the hot pad into a perfect half-circle shape.

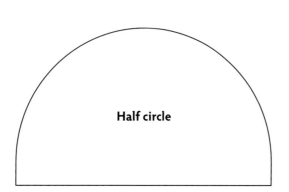

Half circle

Half-circle pattern does not include seam allowances.

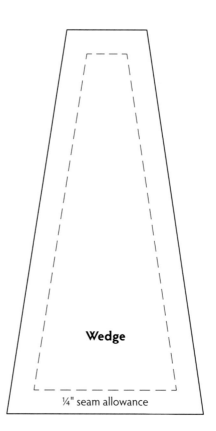

Wedge

¼" seam allowance

Bacon-and-Eggs Hot Pad

No calories in this mouth-watering hot pad! No appliqué either—
just layer, stitch, and cut. This soft and flexible chenille hot pad
will soon become your favorite!

✳ **FINISHED SIZE: 8" diameter** ✳

MATERIALS

*Fat quarters measure 18" × 21". Fat eighths measure
9" × 21". For the solids, choose fabrics that are the
same color on the front and back because both sides
will show in the chenille. Makes 1 hot pad.*

1 fat quarter of turquoise solid for background
1 fat eighth of white solid for egg white and bacon
1 fat quarter of turquoise dot for backing
   and binding
2½" × 21" strip of yellow solid for egg yolk
2½" × 21" strip of red solid for bacon
9" × 9" square of lightweight cotton batting

⅓ yard of 22½"-wide Insul-Bright insulated batting*
Chalk marker or water-soluble marker
Freezer paper for cutting templates
Optional:

✳ Round Up Tool (Creative Grids) for cutting
   circle

✳ Chenille Cutter (Olfa) for cutting stitched
   fabric channels to make chenille

**If you're making multiple hot pads, ⅓ yard of
Insul-Bright is enough to make 2.*

CUTTING

*All strips are cut on the straight grain unless otherwise
noted. Pay attention to the fabric grain! The woven
threads MUST be parallel to the edges of the rotary-
cut pieces or the marked grain lines on the patterns.
To cut the egg shapes, use the patterns on page 15 and
first read "Recycled Cardboard Templates" on page 13.
Use a chalk marker or water-soluble marker to
transfer the grain lines to each egg shape.*

From the turquoise solid, cut:
3 squares, 8" × 8"

From the white solid, cut:
6 egg whites
2 strips, ¼" × 3¾"

From the yellow solid, cut:
4 egg yolks

Continued on page 13

Continued from page 11

From the red solid, cut:

6 strips, 1" × 3¾"

From the turquoise polka dot, cut:

1 rectangle, 8" × 21"; crosscut *on the bias* into
    2½"-wide binding strips to total 30"
2 squares, 9" × 9"

From the Insul-Bright, cut:

1 square, 9" × 9"

* **TERRY'S TIP**

Recycled Cardboard Templates

Trace each pattern shape on page 15 onto
freezer paper and mark the grain lines on
the template. Cut out the paper about ½"
larger than the traced shapes. Iron the
freezer paper, shiny side down, onto
lightweight cardboard such as an old file
folder. Cut out on the line. Use a chalk
marker or water-soluble marker to trace
the templates onto the fabrics.

MAKING THE HOT PAD

1. Stack the three turquoise solid 8" squares and
center them on top of one polka-dot 9" square.
About ½" of the polka-dot print should show all
the way around. Set aside the second polka-dot
9" square for step 6.

2. Mark an 8"-diameter circle on the layered
squares using the pattern on page 15 or the
Round Up Tool (see "Marking Circles with a Ruler"
above right).

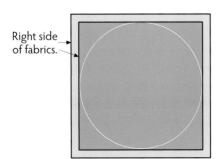

Right side of fabrics.

* **TERRY'S TIP**

Marking Circles with a Ruler

If you want to use the Round Up Tool
rather than a template to cut circles, here's
how. Align the **straight edges** of the Round
Up Tool with the **edges** of the 8" squares.
The drilled hole will be at the center of the
circle. The **4" curve** should be at the upper
corner. Mark along the 4" curve with a
chalk marker or water-soluble marker.
Rotate the square a quarter turn and mark
the second corner using the 4" curve in
the same manner. Repeat at each corner
to make a circle.

3. Make two piles of three egg whites *each* for
the eggs and two piles of three red 1" × 3¾" strips
each for the bacon. Position the stacked pieces
exactly as shown inside the marked circle. The
bacon and eggs should be about ½" from the
circle's edge. Pin. Pay attention—the grain lines
must be parallel to the edges of the square.

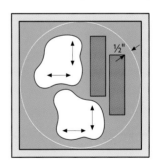

4. Position a white ¼" × 3¾" strip on each piece
of bacon as shown on page 14. Position two
stacked yolks on each egg, making sure the
marked grain lines are parallel to the edges of the
square. Pin. **Pay special attention to the grain
lines in the circles!** You want to keep the threads

of the fabric parallel to the edges of the squares—if the threads are not parallel, your hot pad will ravel and look stringy instead of fluffy.

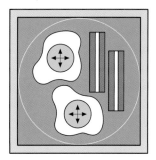

5. Using a water-soluble marker or chalk marker, mark a diagonal line across the stacked pieces from corner to corner.

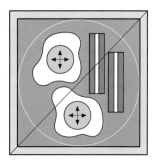

6. Position the remaining polka-dot 9" square on your work surface, wrong side up. Center the Insul-Bright 9" square on top (it doesn't matter which side of the Insul-Bright is facing up). Position the stacked pieces on top of the Insul-Bright, right side up.

7. Using a walking foot, stitch on the marked line through the Insul-Bright and all the fabric layers. Stitch again every ⅜" as shown. Use a stitch length of about 2.5 mm. (There's no need to backstitch.)

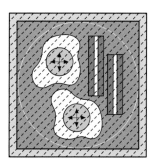

✳ TERRY'S TIP

Quilting the Hot Pad

+ Adjust the needle position, if necessary, so the needle is ⅜" from the edge of your walking foot. Align the edge of the walking foot with the first row of stitching and use it as a guide to stitch the next row.

+ Stitch slowly. Lift the presser foot as needed to avoid catching any of the raw edges.

+ If you have trouble with skipped stitches, switch to a new size 80/12 needle and use lightweight thread such as Aurifil 50-weight.

8. Using a Chenille Cutter or sharp, pointy scissors, cut between each row of stitching as follows. **Do not** cut the polka-dot 9" squares or the Insul-Bright. **Do** cut the stacked shapes and 8" squares. Because the polka-dot layers and Insul-Bright are ½" bigger all the way around the edge, it's easy to insert the cutter or scissors.

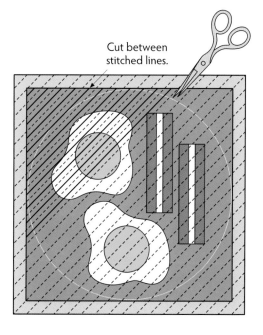

Cut between stitched lines.

9. Cut along the marked circle through all layers using scissors or the Round Up Tool (see "Marking Circles with a Ruler" on page 13; instead of marking, use a rotary cutter to trim the edge).

FINISHING THE HOT PAD

You can download free binding instructions at ShopMartingale.com/HowtoQuilt.

1. Bind using the polka-dot 2½" bias strips.

2. Wash and dry the finished hot pad to fluff up the chenille.

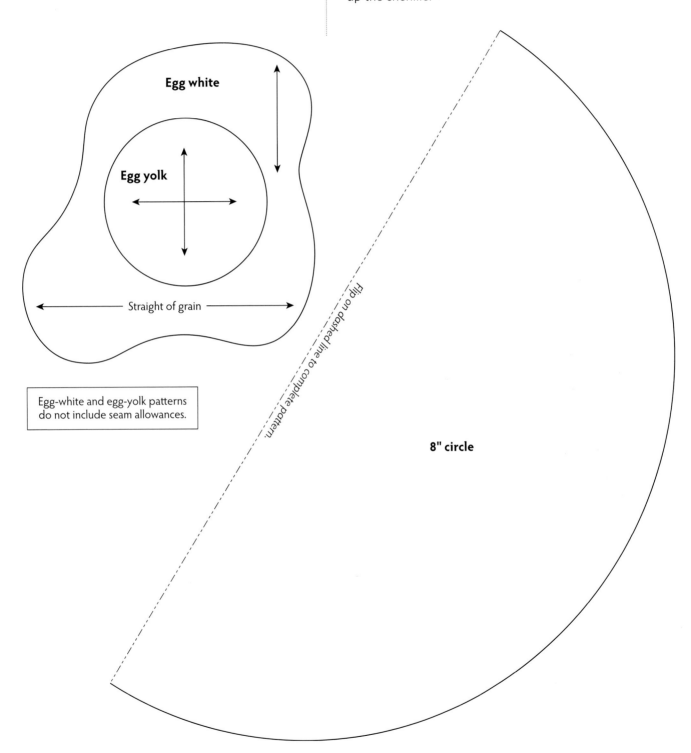

Egg white

Egg yolk

Straight of grain

Flip on dashed line to complete pattern.

Egg-white and egg-yolk patterns do not include seam allowances.

8" circle

Color Block Table Topper

Four quarters in a dollar, four quarts in a gallon, and four fat quarters in this reversible table runner. The prints are used on both the front and the back, so there's nothing left over!

✳ **FINISHED SIZE: 13½" × 38½"** ✳

MATERIALS

Yardage is based on 42"-wide fabric unless otherwise noted. Fat quarters measure 18" × 21".

4 fat quarters of assorted prints for table-topper top and backing
⅜ yard of navy print for sashing and binding
18" × 40" rectangle of lightweight cotton batting
Optional: Magic Sizing or Mary Ellen's Best Press

CUTTING

From *each of 2* of the fat quarters, cut:
1 strip, 9½" × 21" (2 total)
1 strip, 8" × 21" (2 total)

From *each of the 2 remaining* fat quarters, cut:
1 strip, 13" × 21" (2 total)
1 strip, 4½" × 21" (2 total)

From the navy print, cut:
3 strips, 2¼" × 42"
5 strips, 1½" × 13½"

✳ **TERRY'S TIP**

Press for Success

Press all fabric using Magic Sizing or Mary Ellen's Best Press before you cut. It will make the fabric crisp and easy to work with!

MAKING THE TABLE TOPPER

Use a ¼"-wide seam allowance throughout.

1. Stitch each 4½" × 21" strip to a 9½" × 21" strip along a long edge. Press the seam allowances toward the narrower strip. Each strip set should measure 13½" × 21".

2. From *each* strip set, cut one 8"-wide segment, one 6"-wide segment, and one 4"-wide segment.

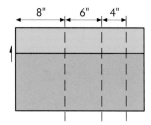

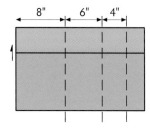

Make 1 of each strip set.
Cut 1 of each segment from each.

3. Arrange the segments as shown above right, alternating colors and rotating every other unit to position the small rectangles along opposite edges. Place the navy 1½" × 13½" strips between the units. Stitch the units and strips together to

make the table-topper top. Press the seam allowances toward the strips. The runner top should measure 13½" × 38½".

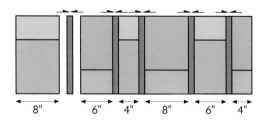

FINISHING THE TABLE TOPPER

You can download free finishing instructions at ShopMartingale.com/HowtoQuilt.

1. To make the backing, sew the 8" × 21" and 13" × 21" strips together as shown. Press all the seam allowances in the same direction. The backing should measure 21" × 40½".

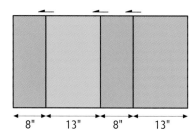

2. Layer the table topper with batting and backing. Quilt as desired by hand or machine.

3. Bind the table topper's edges using the navy 2¼" × 42" strips.

Sling Bag

What kind of prints will you mix and match in this fat-quarter bag?
To make it extra special, hand dye custom colors or embellish
with embroidery or buttons.

✳ **FINISHED SIZE: 11½" × 16" × 4½", excluding handle** ✳

MATERIALS

Yardage is based on 42"-wide fabric unless otherwise noted. Fat quarters measure 18" × 21".

4 fat quarters of assorted prints (pink, coral, turquoise, and green) for bag front, back, bottom, handle, pockets, and button loop

⅔ yard of muslin for interlining (This will be used to stabilize the bag and will not show.)

1 yard of turquoise print for lining (This will show inside the bag.)

14"-long coil zipper

1 button, ⅞" diameter

Freezer paper for cutting template

CUTTING

From *each* assorted print, refer to the diagram below to cut:
1 rectangle, 8½" × 16½" (4 total; bag front and back)
2 rectangles, 5" × 7½" (8 total; handle and bag front)

From the remaining print scraps, cut a *total* of:
1 strip, 5" × 16½" (bag bottom)
2 squares, 5" × 5" (bag front and back)
1 strip, 1½" × 5" (button loop)

From the muslin, cut:
1 strip, 16½" × 42"
1 strip, 5" × 42"

From the turquoise print, cut:
1 strip, 16½" × 42"; crosscut into:
    1 rectangle, 16½" × 26"
    1 rectangle, 5" × 16½"
1 strip, 8½" × 42"; crosscut into:
    3 squares, 8½" × 8½"
    2 rectangles, 4½" × 8½"
1 strip, 5" × 42"

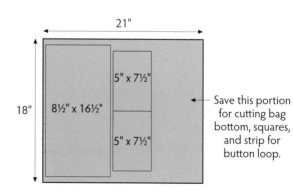

21"

18"

8½" x 16½"

5" x 7½"

5" x 7½"

Save this portion for cutting bag bottom, squares, and strip for button loop.

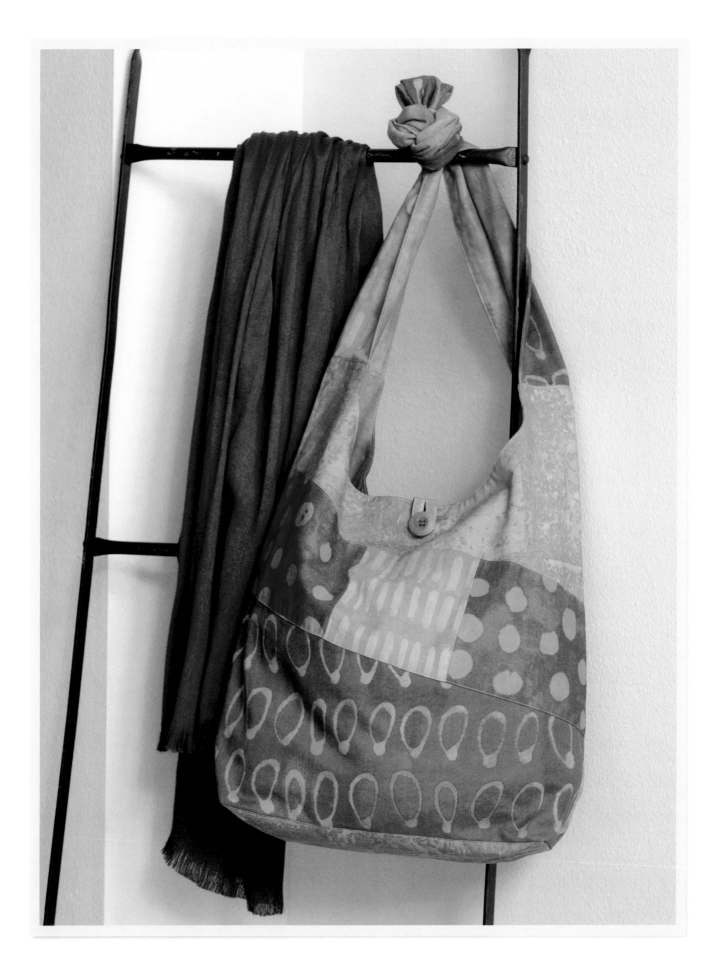

MAKING THE BAG FRONT, BACK, AND HANDLE

Use a ¼"-wide seam allowance throughout unless otherwise noted.

1. Sew together two print 8½" × 16½" rectangles along the long edge to make the bag front. Press the seam allowances toward the darker fabric. The bag front should measure 16½" square.

2. Stitch a print 5" square between two print 5" × 7½" rectangles as shown. Press the seam allowances open. Press under ¼" along each long edge of the pieced strip.

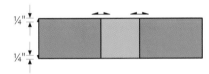

3. Place the pieced strip, right side up, diagonally across the bag front so it covers the seam; pin. Trim the ends even. Topstitch all the way around the strip as shown, stitching close to the edge.

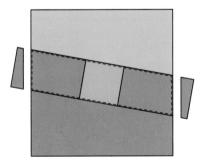

Topstitch.

4. Sew together the two remaining print 8½" × 16½" rectangles along the long edge to make the bag back.

5. Press under ¼" along all the edges of the remaining print 5" square. Center the square over the bag-back seam. Topstitch all the way around the square as shown, stitching close to the edge.

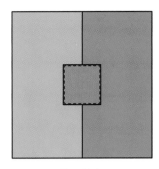

Topstitch.

6. Sew the print 5" × 16½" strip between the bag front and back. Press the seam allowances toward the 5" strip.

7. Pin the unit, right side up, on top of the muslin 16½" × 42" strip. Topstitch through both layers all the way around, close to the edge. Trim the muslin even with the edges of the pieced rectangle to make the bag-body panel.

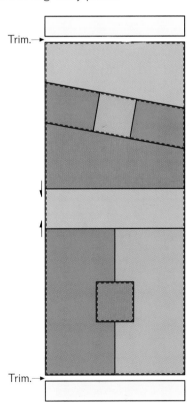

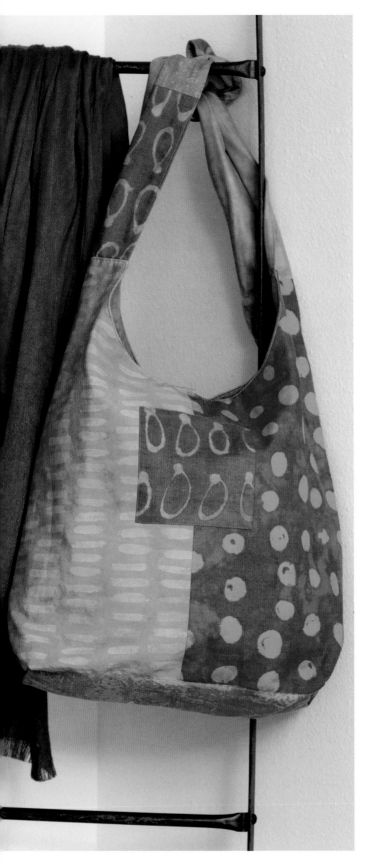

✳ *A contrasting accent square makes the back of the bag as attractive as the front.*

8. Trace the half-oval pattern (page 27) onto freezer paper and cut out on the outer drawn lines to make a template. Fold the short ends of the bag-body panel in half and put a pin at the fold to mark the center of the bag-body panel. Matching centers, position and trace around the half-oval template at each short end of the bag body panel. Stitch along the marked lines.

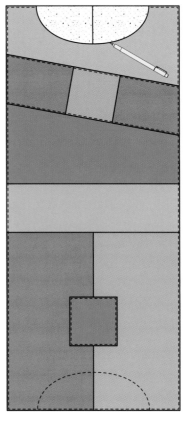

Stitch on line.

9. Sew together the six remaining print 5" × 7½" rectangles end to end. Press the seam allowances in one direction. The pieced strip should measure 5" × 42½".

10. Center and pin the pieced strip, right side up, on top of the muslin 5" × 42" strip. Stitch through both layers on both long edges, close to the edge. Trim the pieced rectangle even with the edges of the muslin to make the handle panel.

Trim.

11. If desired, decorate your bag panel and handle panel with embroidery.

12. Pin the handle panel to the turquoise 5" × 42" strip with right sides together and stitch along both long edges. Turn right side out. Press. Topstitch close to the edges all the way around to make the handle.

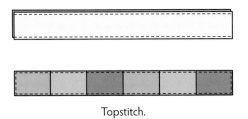

Topstitch.

MAKING THE LINING, POCKET, AND LOOP

1. Layer two turquoise 8½" squares right sides together with the edges even. Slide a zipper **between** the top edges of the squares with the zipper pull facing down. The edge of the zipper tape and raw edges of the squares should be even. Stitch as shown through all layers.

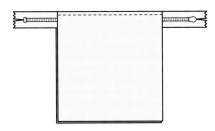

2. Turn the unit right sides out. Finger-press both squares away from the zipper teeth. Topstitch close to the fold along the zipper as shown to make the zipper panel.

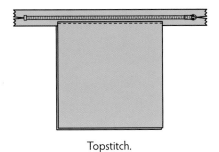

Topstitch.

3. Pin the zipper panel, right side up, on top of the remaining turquoise 8½" square, right side up. The top of the zipper tape should be even with the top edge of the square. The bottom edges will not be even. Stitch a scant ¼" along the top edges.

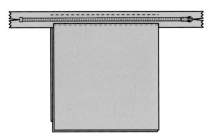

4. Trim the bottom edges even. **Move the zipper pull to the center** so you don't cut it off. Stitch ⅛" from the bottom and side edges, through all layers, to make the pocket. Trim the zipper ends even with the pocket sides.

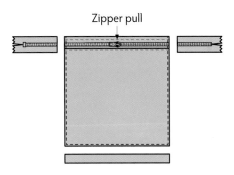

Zipper pull

5. Stitch a turquoise 4½" × 8½" rectangle to each side of the pocket. Press the seam allowances away from the pocket. (Try not to touch the zipper with the iron.) Topstitch through all layers close to each seam.

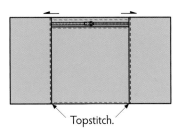

Topstitch.

6. Sew the turquoise 5" × 16½" rectangle to the top edge of the pocket panel and the turquoise 16½" × 26" rectangle to the bottom edge of the pocket panel to make the lining panel. Topstitch through all layers close to each seam.

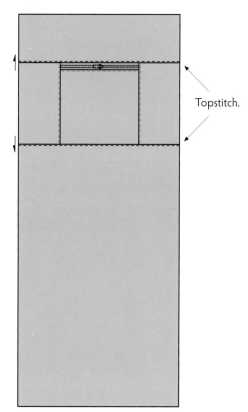

Topstitch.

7. Press the print 1½" × 5" strip in half lengthwise with wrong sides together. Open the strip and then fold the raw edges in to meet at the center crease. Press. Refold along the center crease and press. Topstitch along the long edges close to the fold to make the button loop.

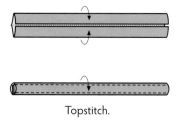

Topstitch.

8. Mark the center of the strip. On each side of the center point, fold the ends under to form a point as shown above right. Stitch a line back

and forth through all layers to secure. Stitch another line as shown to make a loop that's ⅛" larger than your button.

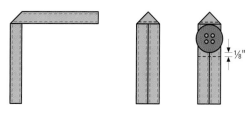

⅛"

ASSEMBLING THE BAG

1. Place the turquoise panel wrong side up on your work surface. Position the bag-body panel, right side up, on top of the turquoise panel with top edges even. Trim the lining panel even with the bag-body panel. Trim the curve at each end (both layers), about ⅛" outside the curved stitching line. **Do not sew yet!** Set aside the lining panel.

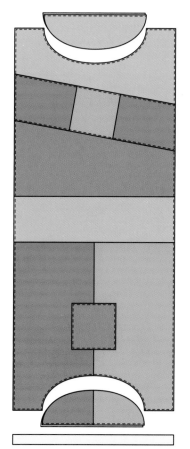

Layer and trim.

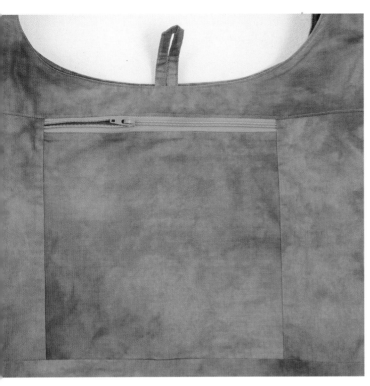

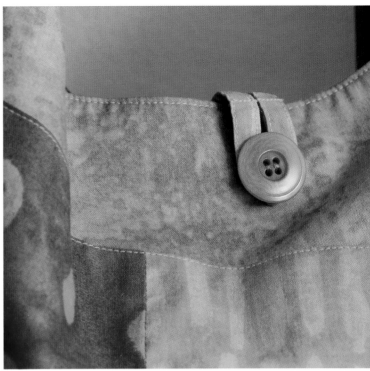

2. Center the button loop on the bag back as shown with raw edges even. Stitch across the button loop a scant ¼" from the raw edges.

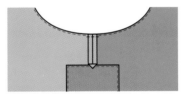

3. Fold the bag-body panel in half, right sides together. Stitch along the side edges, backstitching at the beginning and end of the seams. Press the seam allowances toward the bag back.

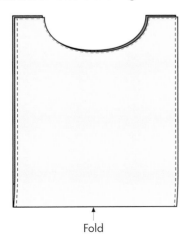

Fold

4. With the bag body still wrong side out, fold each bottom corner as shown. Mark a line perpendicular to the side seam, 2¼" from the corner. Stitch on the line through all layers, backstitching at the beginning and end of the seams. This will make the bottom of the bag flat.

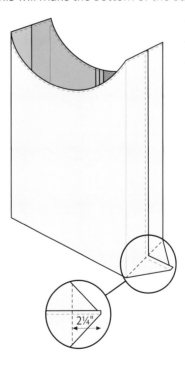

2¼"

5. With right sides together and raw edges even, pin the handle to the top edge of the bag body. Center each end of the handle over a side seam. Stitch a scant ¼" seam as shown. (See "Terry's Tip" on page 27.)

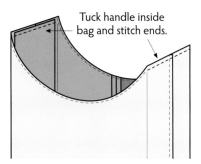

Tuck handle inside bag and stitch ends.

6. Fold the lining panel in half, right sides together. Stitch along the side edges, leaving a 10" opening in one side and backstitching at the beginning and end of each seam. Press the seam allowances toward the lining front (the side without the pocket).

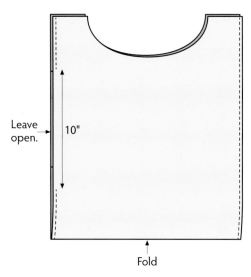

Leave open.

10"

Fold

7. With the lining still wrong side out, repeat step 4 with the lining.

8. Turn the lining right side out. Put the lining inside the outer bag with raw edges even and right sides together. Make sure the zipper pocket is facing the bag back! Pin. Stitch. Stop with the needle down and pivot at each end of the curve.

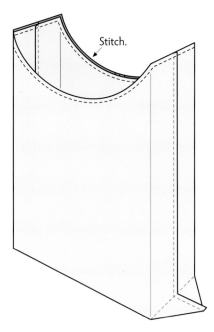

Stitch.

9. Clip the seam allowances along each curve. Turn the bag right side out, pulling it through the 10" opening in the lining seam. Insert the lining into the bag and press the top edge flat. Topstitch a scant ¼" from the edge. Stitch the opening in the lining by hand or machine to close it.

10. Stitch the button to the front of the bag. And enjoy!

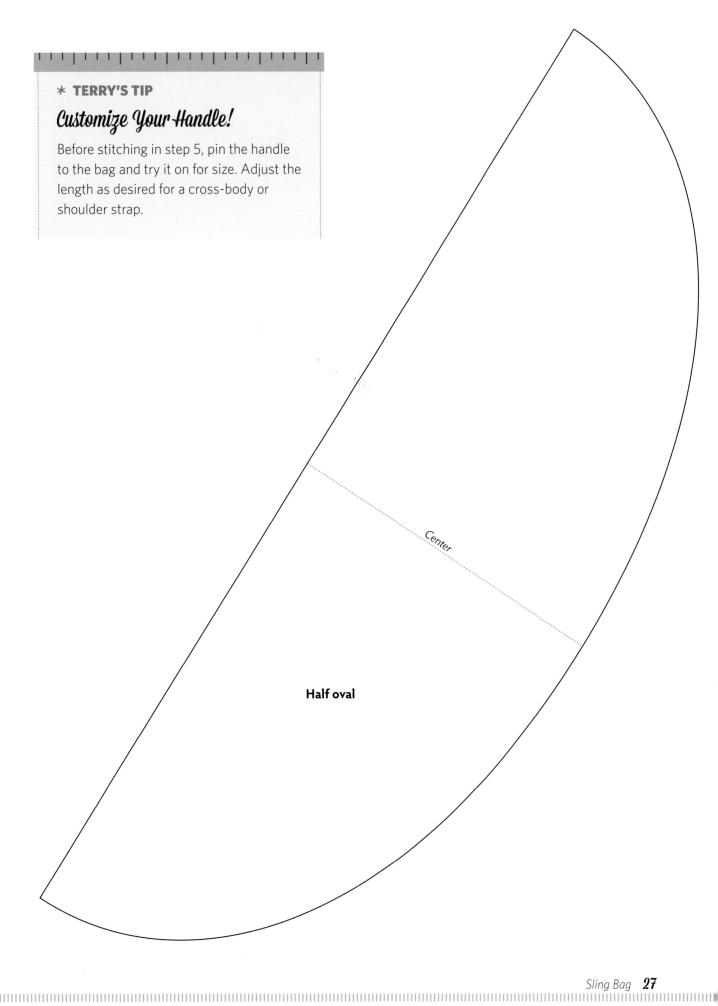

Customize Your Handle!

Before stitching in step 5, pin the handle to the bag and try it on for size. Adjust the length as desired for a cross-body or shoulder strap.

Center

Half oval

Buttoned Napkin Holders

Make a holder in holiday colors or to coordinate with your everyday dishes. Perfect for parties and gift giving! Heading out to a quilt retreat? These cute and collapsible holders are great for catching threads while you sew.

MATERIALS

Yardage is based on 42"-wide fabric unless otherwise noted. Fat quarters measure 18" × 21". Makes 1 napkin holder in any of the listed sizes or 1 tea-bag holder.

2 fat quarters of coordinating prints (yellow fruit print and green dot for napkin holder or red floral and green print for tea-bag holder)

¾ yard of 20"-wide woven fusible interfacing, such as Pellon SF101

½ yard of ultrafirm, heavyweight fusible stabilizer, such as Peltex 71F (Pellon)

4 buttons, ¾" diameter (for any napkin holder), or 4 buttons, ½" diameter (for tea-bag holder)

4 skinny hair elastics

Appliqué pressing sheet or pressing cloth to protect iron when fusing

Fray Check seam sealant

Optional:

* Stiletto to help hold the edges as you stitch
* Wonder Clips (Clover) for securing multiple layers of fabric and interfacing

FINISHED SIZES:

Cocktail-napkin holder: 5½" × 5½" × 2½" (fits 5" × 5" napkins)

Luncheon-napkin holder: 7" × 7" × 2½" (fits 6½" × 6½" napkins)

Rectangular-napkin holder: 5" × 8½" × 2½" (fits 4½" × 8" napkins)

Tea-bag or sugar-packet holder: 2½" × 3½" × 2"

Make Them All!

If you want to make all four of the different napkin holders, here's what you'll need:

+ ½ yard *each* of 3 coordinating prints
+ 2 yards of 20"-wide woven fusible interfacing
+ 1½ yards of ultrafirm, heavyweight fusible stabilizer
+ 16 buttons
+ 16 skinny hair elastics

CUTTING FOR THE COCKTAIL-NAPKIN HOLDER

From the yellow fruit print, cut:
1 square, 12" × 12"

From the green dot, cut:
1 square, 12" × 12"

From the fusible interfacing, cut;
2 squares, 11½" × 11½"

From the Peltex, cut:
2 squares, 5½" × 5½"
8 rectangles, 2½" × 5½"

CUTTING FOR THE LUNCHEON-NAPKIN HOLDER

From the yellow fruit print, cut:
1 square, 13½" × 13½"

From the green dot, cut:
1 square, 13½" × 13½"

From the fusible interfacing, cut;
2 squares, 13" × 13"

From the Peltex, cut:
2 squares, 7" × 7"
8 rectangles, 2½" × 7"

CUTTING FOR THE RECTANGULAR-NAPKIN HOLDER

From the yellow fruit print, cut:
1 rectangle, 11½" × 15"

From the green dot, cut:
1 rectangle, 11½" × 15"

From the fusible interfacing, cut;
2 rectangles, 11" × 14½"

From the Peltex, cut:
2 rectangles, 5" × 8½"
4 rectangles, 2½" × 8½"
4 rectangles, 2½" × 5"

CUTTING FOR THE TEA-BAG HOLDER

From the red floral, cut:
1 rectangle, 8" × 9"

From the green print, cut:
1 rectangle, 8" × 9"

From the fusible interfacing, cut;
2 rectangles, 7½" × 8½"

From the Peltex, cut:
2 rectangles, 2½" × 3½"
4 rectangles, 2" × 3½"
4 rectangles, 2" × 2½"

★ TERRY'S TIP

Covered Buttons

Make fabric-covered buttons if you can't find matching buttons in the right size. Use a purchased button-cover kit and follow the package directions. If you don't have a kit, use a button and a fabric scrap to make your own custom button. Cut a fabric circle slightly smaller than twice the diameter of the button. Using a hand-sewing needle and quilting thread, stitch a running stitch around the edge of the circle. Pull the thread ends to gather the edges and insert the button. Pull tight and knot the threads behind the button.

MAKING THE HOLDER

These instructions work for any of the napkin or tea-bag holder sizes.

1. Following the manufacturer's instructions, center and fuse one interfacing square or rectangle to the wrong side of the green-dot square or rectangle.

2. Center and fuse one of the largest Peltex pieces to the interfacing side of the green-dot fabric. Use an appliqué pressing sheet to protect your iron.

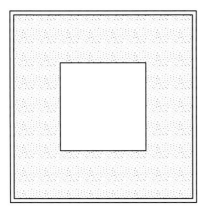

3. Fuse four of the smaller Peltex rectangles around the center as shown, leaving ⅛" between the pieces.

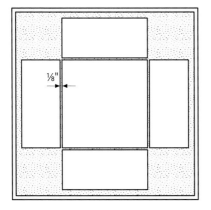

✳ TERRY'S TIP

The Perfect Space

Stand an acrylic ruler up perpendicular to the fabric and use the ruler's edge as a spacer to position the pieces evenly.

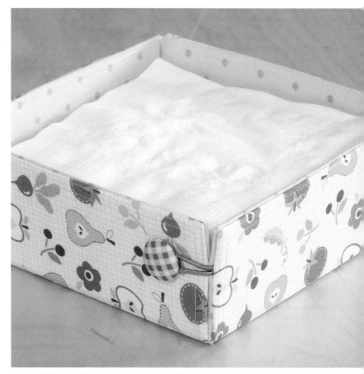

✳ *Button closures are both eye-catching and functional.*

4. Trim away a square of fabric at each corner, ¾" from the Peltex. Clip the inner corners up to the Peltex.

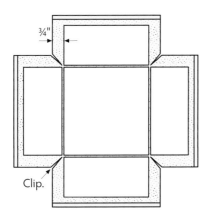

5. Stitch a rectangle that's ¼" from the edge of the Peltex, folding the fabric edges around the edge of the Peltex as you go. Stitch the second rectangle, turning over the remaining edges.

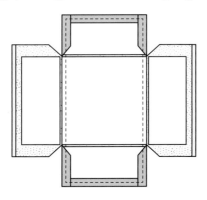

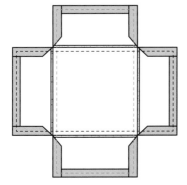

★ TERRY'S TIP

Pin Alternative

I like to use a stiletto instead of pins to hold the fabric edges in place as I sew.

6. Repeat steps 1–5 with the fruit print and the remaining fusible interfacing and Peltex pieces.

7. Position the hair elastics 1" from alternating corners on the green-dot unit as shown (if you're making the tea-bag holder, position them ¾" from alternating corners). The elastic loop should extend 1" beyond the edge (or ¾" for the tea-bag holder). Using a short stitch length, stitch a few times across the elastic on top of the previous stitching line.

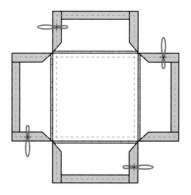

8. Layer the fruit-print and green-dot units with edges even and wrong sides together. Stitch close to the edge, a scant ¼" from the previous stitching lines. Stitch through all layers.

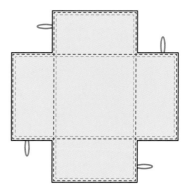

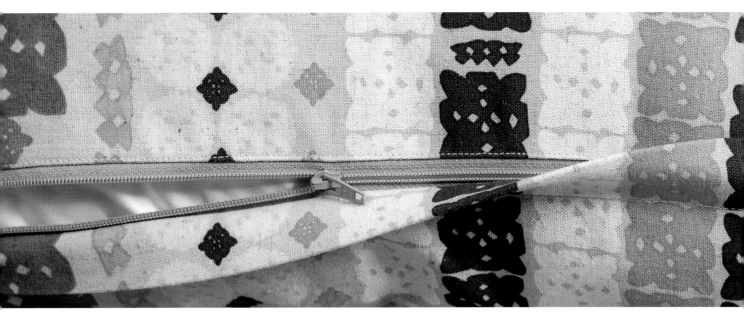

* *A lapped closure hides the zipper teeth, keeping both sides of your pillow display-worthy.*

2. Center the trimmed zipper on the bottom edge of the upper-back rectangle, right sides together and zipper pull facing down. Using a zipper foot, stitch a ¼" seam.

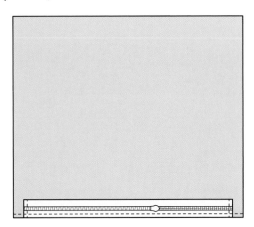

* **TERRY'S TIP**

Stitching Past the Zipper Pull

Stitch along the zipper tape until you reach the zipper pull. Stop with the needle down. Lift the presser foot and slide the zipper pull out of the way. Continue stitching to the end.

3. Fold the fabric away from the zipper and topstitch close to the fold through all layers.

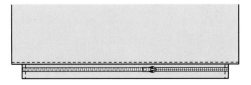

4. Press under 1¼" along the top edge of the lower-back rectangle. Mark a line 1" from each end, perpendicular to the fold. Draw a line between the marks, 1" from and parallel to the fold, exactly as shown.

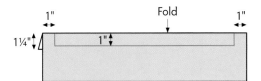

5. Unfold the crease. Place the upper-back unit on top of the lower-back unit with right sides together. The edge of the zipper tape should be even with the raw edge of the marked panel. Stitch a ¼" seam.

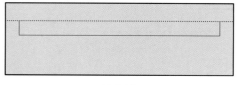

Unfold.

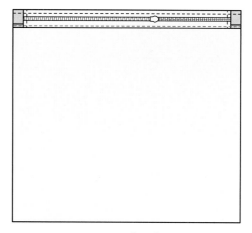

Layer and stitch.

6. Refold the crease. Beginning at the edge, use a zipper foot to stitch close to the fold up to the marked line. Pivot and stitch along the marked lines as shown. Pivot and stitch along the fold to the end to make the pillow back panel.

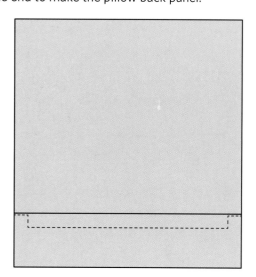

✳ **TERRY'S TIP**

Backstitch to Secure

In step 6, reinforce the vertical line of stitching by backstitching at the fold.

7. To round the pillow corners, place the pillow front on top of the back panel. Trim if needed so the front and back are exactly the same size. Mark a curve at each corner using the corner pattern provided on page 39 or the Curved Corner Cutter (2" radius corner). Trim the corners on the marked lines. **Do not sew together yet!**

✳ **TERRY'S TIP**

Pantry Substitute

A round tin can of tuna or vegetables or a cup will work to round the corner. The size doesn't matter—we're just eliminating the pillow's pointy corners. Why not use your rotary cutter to trim around a tin can?

MAKING AND ADDING THE PIPING

1. Sew the multicolored 1¾"-wide bias strips together using diagonal seams to make one long bias strip. Press the seam allowances open. Fold one short end under ½" and press.

2. Starting about an inch from the pressed end, wrap the bias strip around the cotton cording. If using cotton cord, stitch close to the cord with a zipper foot on your machine. If using Wrap 'n Fuse, press just the seam allowances to fuse the strip in place.

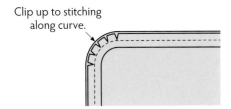

3. With raw edges even, stitch the piping to the right side of just the **pillow front** close to the cord. Clip the piping seam allowances, stopping just before the stitching, as needed to ease the piping around the curved corners.

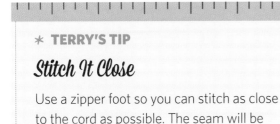

Clip up to stitching along curve.

4. When you reach the starting point, trim the end of the piping so the ends butt up against each other. Tuck the end into the overlapping fabric at the beginning and finish stitching.

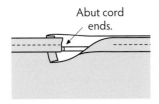

Abut cord ends.

✳ **TERRY'S TIP**

Stitch It Close

Use a zipper foot so you can stitch as close to the cord as possible. The seam will be wider than ¼".

✳ *Fabric-covered cording adds professional panache to these pillows.*

FINISHING THE PILLOW

1. **Unzip the zipper halfway.** Pin the pillow front and pillow back together, right sides together. (Or use Clover Wonder Clips to hold the pillow front and back together.) Using a zipper foot, stitch all the way around the pillow. Stitch with the pillow front on top so that you can sew just inside the previous line of stitching.

2. Turn the pillow cover right side out and insert a pillow form.

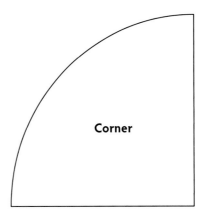

Corner

Taffy Twists Throw Pillow

Add some texture to the front of a 16" pillow with easy-to-sew twisted fabric tubes. Make the twists a lighter color for subtle contrast.

✳ **FINISHED SIZE: 16" × 16"** ✳

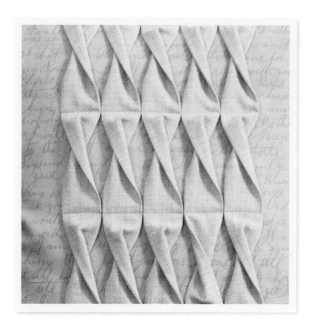

MATERIALS

Yardage is based on 42"-wide fabric unless otherwise noted. Fat quarters measure 18" × 21".

1 yard of teal print A for pillow front, pillow back, and piping

1 fat quarter of teal print B for twists

1⅜ yards of 20"-wide woven fusible interfacing, such as Pellon SF101

2 yards of ¼" cotton cord for piping

16" × 16" pillow form

22"-long coil zipper

Zipper foot

Chalk marker or water-soluble marker

Optional: Wrap 'n Fuse (Clover) for easily making piping (If you use this, don't purchase the ¼" cotton cord for piping.)

CUTTING

Referring to the cutting instructions for the 16" × 16" pillow on page 36, cut and interface the teal print A pieces for the pillow front, upper back, lower back, and piping.

From teal print B, cut:

5 strips, 3" × 21"

MAKING THE PILLOW COVER

Use a ¼"-wide seam allowance throughout, unless otherwise noted. Use the interfaced 16½" × 16½" pillow front in the following steps.

1. Fold each teal print B 3" × 21" strip in half lengthwise, right sides together, and stitch a ¼" seam along the long edge. Turn right side out and press flat with the seam along one edge.

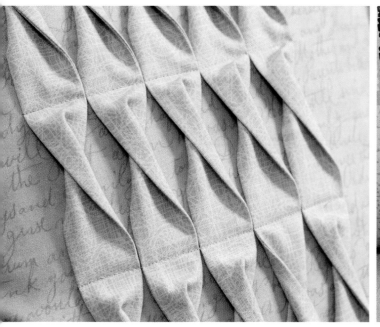

2. Using a chalk marker or water-soluble marker, mark a vertical line along the center of the pillow front. Mark two additional lines on each side of the centerline, 1¼" apart. Mark horizontal lines as shown ¾" from the top and bottom edges. Starting at the top horizontal line, mark four evenly spaced horizontal lines 3" apart as shown.

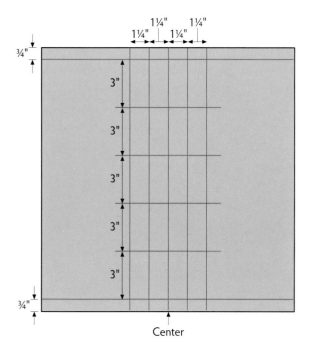

Center

3. With the top raw edges even, center a strip over each vertical line on the pillow front. Stitch across the strips, ¾" from the top edge of the pillow. Backstitch at the beginning and end.

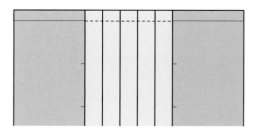

4. Twist each strip once and stitch across them at the first 3" line. Repeat at each 3" line. Your last row of stitching will be ¾" from the bottom edge. Trim the strips even with the bottom edge.

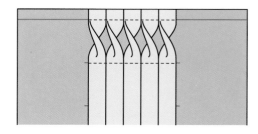

FINISHING THE PILLOW

Add piping and finish your pillow following the instructions in the Pillow Talk project (page 36).

Sewing Supplies Pocket Roll-Up

Organize your hand-sewing and embroidery supplies for when you're on the go. Choose a curved or angled flap in two sizes. Get creative— customize your pockets and decorate the flap!

⁂ **FINISHED SIZES: Large: 8" × 10½" (open); 8" × 4" (closed) Small: 6" × 10½" (open); 6" × 4" (closed)** ⁂

MATERIALS

Fat quarters measure 18" × 21". Makes 1 roll-up of either size.

1 fat quarter for body of roll-up (pink batik for small size *OR* multicolored print for large size)

1 fat quarter of accent fabric for binding and pocket lining (yellow batik for small size *OR* aqua print for large size)

⅝ yard of 20"-wide woven fusible interfacing, such as Pellon SF101

14"-long coil zipper (it will be trimmed to size)

¾" square of Velcro for closure

1 button, 1" diameter, for embellishment

Zipper foot

Freezer paper for cutting template

CUTTING

All strips are cut on the straight grain unless otherwise noted. Pieces are assigned letter labels for clarity.

For the Small Roll-Up

From the pink batik, cut:

1 strip, 10½" × 21"; crosscut into:
    2 rectangles, 6" × 10½" (A)
    1 rectangle, 1¼" × 6" (B)
1 strip, 7" × 21"; crosscut into:
    1 rectangle, 6" × 7" (C)
    2 rectangles, 3" × 6" (D)

From the yellow batik, cut:

2 strips, 2¼" × 20" or longer, *on the bias*
2 rectangles, 3¾" × 6" (E)

From the fusible interfacing, cut:

1 strip, 10½" × 20"; crosscut into 2 rectangles, 6" × 10½" (A)
1 strip, 3½" × 20"; crosscut into 1 rectangle, 3½" × 6" (F)
1 strip, 3" × 20"; crosscut into 2 rectangles, 3" × 6" (D)
1 strip, 2¾" × 20"; crosscut into 2 rectangles, 2¾" × 6" (G)

Continued on page 45

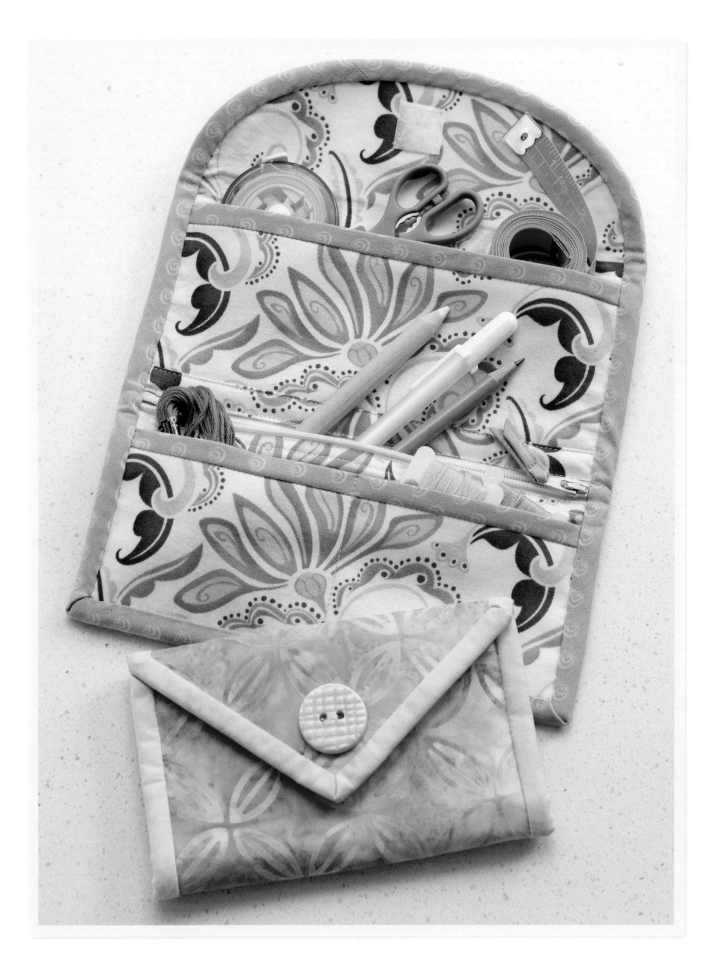

Continued from page 43

For the Large Roll-Up

From the multicolored print, cut:

1 strip, 10½" × 21"; crosscut into:
    2 rectangles, 8" × 10½" (A)
    1 rectangle, 1¼" × 8" (B)
1 strip, 7" × 21"; crosscut into:
    1 rectangle, 7" × 8" (C)
    2 rectangles, 3" × 8" (D)

From the aqua print, cut:

2 strips, 2¼" × 20" or longer, *on the bias*
2 rectangles, 3¾" × 8" (E)

From the fusible interfacing, cut:

1 strip, 10½" × 20"; crosscut into 2 rectangles,
    8" × 10½" (A)
1 strip, 3½" × 20"; crosscut into 1 rectangle,
    3½" × 8" (F)
1 strip, 3" × 20"; crosscut into 2 rectangles,
    3" × 8" (D)
1 strip, 2¾" × 20"; crosscut into 2 rectangles,
    2¾" × 8" (G)

MAKING THE ROLL-UP

Use a ¼"-wide seam allowance throughout, unless otherwise noted.

1. Following the manufacturer's instructions, center and fuse an interfacing A rectangle to the wrong side of each fabric A rectangle. To stabilize the flap, fuse an interfacing G rectangle at one end of each rectangle. Make two.

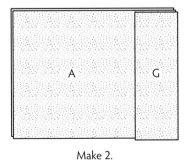

Make 2.

(both on page 48)

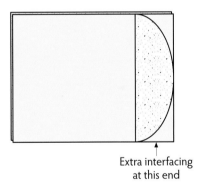

⋆ **TERRY'S TIP**

Keep Your Iron Free from Residue

I like to place a press cloth between the iron and fabric as I press, to make sure I don't get any adhesive on my iron. Any lightweight cotton fabric will work for this purpose.

2. Stack the rectangles, keeping wrong sides together and the extra interfacing at the same end. For a curved flap, trace the 8" curved flap pattern for the large roll-up or the 6" curved flap pattern for the small roll-up (both on page 48) onto freezer paper and cut out on the drawn lines to make a template. Position the flap template on the stacked rectangles at the end with the extra interfacing. Trace around the curved edge on the right side of the fabric. For an angled flap, mark lines as shown at the end with the extra interfacing.

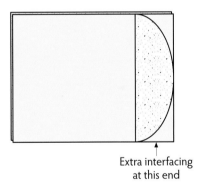

Extra interfacing
at this end

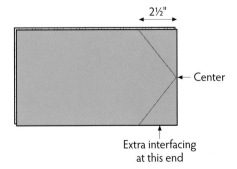

2½"

Center

Extra interfacing
at this end

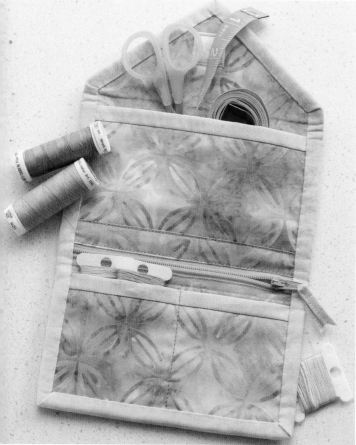

3. Sew all the way around the stacked rectangles, about ⅛" from the edge, stitching just inside the marked line. To shape the flap, trim a curve or an angle along the marked lines.

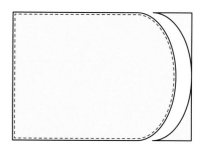

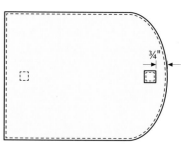

4. Center the loop side of the Velcro square ¾" from the flap edge and stitch it in place. **Flip the panel over.** Center the hook side of the Velcro at the opposite end. Before sewing the second Velcro piece in place, **fold the panel in thirds and test to make sure you have positioned the Velcro correctly!** After confirming that the placement is correct, stitch the second piece of Velcro in place.

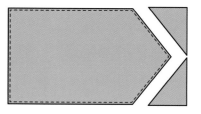

¾"

5. To make the zipper pocket, fuse the interfacing F rectangle onto the wrong side of the fabric C rectangle as shown. Fold the fabric rectangle in half with wrong sides together and press. The pocket should measure 3½" × 8" (large) or 3½" × 6" (small).

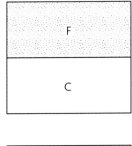

6. Place the pocket over the zipper, centering the zipper and placing the pocket fold ⅛" from the zipper teeth. **The zipper pull should face up.** Using a zipper foot, stitch close to the fold. Stitch again a scant ¼" away, being sure you're still catching the edge of the zipper tape below. Do not trim the zipper yet!

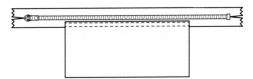

7. To make the pockets with a contrasting edge, fuse an interfacing D rectangle to the wrong side of each fabric D rectangle. Sew an accent-fabric E rectangle to each D rectangle along the long edge. Press the seam allowances toward the accent fabric. Wrap the accent fabric around the seam allowances to the back of piece D, matching the bottom edges, and press flat to form the pocket lining and a contrasting edge at the top of the pocket. Stitch in the ditch close to the accent fabric. Make two.

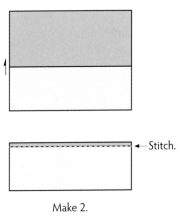

Make 2.

8. Fold the fabric B rectangle in half and press to mark the center. Unfold. Press under both long edges of the rectangle so that the raw edges meet at the center.

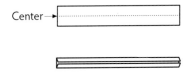

9. Place a pocket with a contrasting edge on top of the zipper pocket as shown, with raw edges even. Pin. Mark a vertical stitching line at the center of the pocket. Stitch on the line through all layers. Backstitch at the beginning and end. See "Terry's Tip" at left.

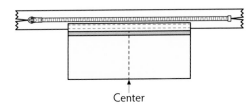

Center

10. Place the layered pockets on the panel from step 4, raw edges even as shown and right sides up. Stitch along the sides and bottom edge, ⅛" from the edge through all the layers. Do not stitch across the zipper!

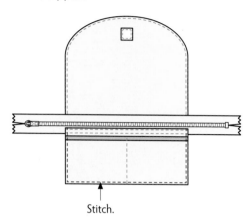

Stitch.

11. Place the remaining pocket with a contrasting edge above the zipper, with the raw edge touching the edge of the zipper tape.

12. Position the strip from step 8 over the pocket's lower edge as shown, ⅛" from the zipper teeth and right side up. Using a zipper foot, stitch close to both long edges through all layers.

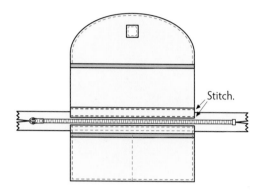

Stitch.

13. Move the zipper pull to the center. Stitch ⅛" from the roll-up's side edges, stitching across the zipper. **Make sure the zipper pull is inside the stitching.** Trim the zipper ends.

FINISHING THE ROLL-UP

You can download free binding instructions at ShopMartingale.com/HowtoQuilt.

1. Stitch the 2¼" accent-fabric strips together using a diagonal seam. Press the long binding strip in half lengthwise, wrong sides together. Stitch the binding to the outside of the roll-up, using a ¼" seam. Fold the binding around the edge and stitch it in place by hand.

2. Stitch the button onto the right side of the flap, above the Velcro.

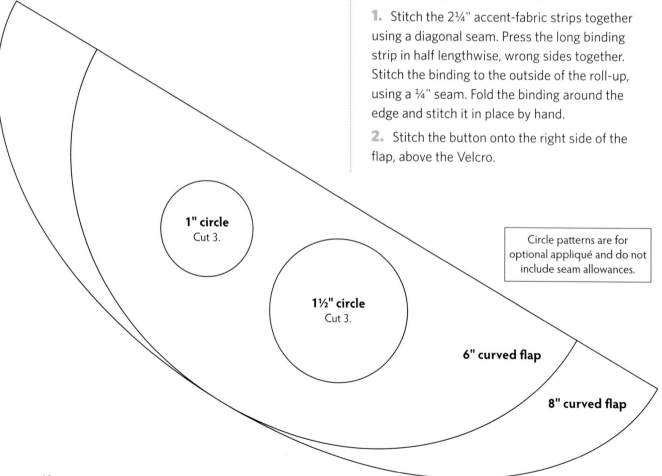

1" circle
Cut 3.

1½" circle
Cut 3.

Circle patterns are for optional appliqué and do not include seam allowances.

6" curved flap

8" curved flap

✂ Creative Options

Try using wool, flannel, or a textured fabric for the outside layer of your roll-up. Fuse the interfacing as usual.

Make a decorative zipper pull. Cut a 1" × 4" strip from leftover fabric. Fold it in half lengthwise, wrong sides together, and press. Tuck the raw edges in and press again (if you offset the folded edges a tiny bit, you'll be sure to catch the bottom layer while stitching). Topstitch along the edge through both folds, being sure to hang on to your threads to help get the stitching started. Because this strip is so skinny, it will be really hard to stitch straight at the ends; that's OK, because you'll cut the ends off! Cut one end at an angle and thread it through the zipper pull. Fold it in half and stitch across as shown. Trim the ends to the desired length at an angle.

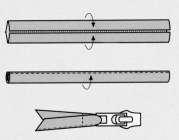

Add a window pocket. Use a clear plastic pocket instead of one of the pockets with a contrasting edge. Using Quilter's Vinyl or clear plastic, cut 1 strip, 3" × 8" (large) or 3" × 6" (small). For the pocket binding, cut 1 strip, 1½" × 8" (large) or 1½" × 6" (small). Fold the binding in half lengthwise, wrong sides together, and press. Open and press both edges in to meet at the center crease. Refold the center crease and press again. Slide the clear vinyl rectangle into the binding and stitch through all layers.

Customize the size. For a customized roll-up, make your roll-up 1" wider than the length of your scissors so the scissors will easily fit in the pocket.

Add wool or fleece for needle storage. Center a 1½" × 4" piece of wool or fleece on top of one pocket in step 7. Stitch in place.

Decorate the flap. To add appliqué to the flap, trace the 1½" circle pattern and 1" circle pattern (page 48) onto freezer paper and cut out on the drawn lines to make templates. Use the templates to cut three 1½" circles and three 1" circles from felt or felted wool. Referring to the photo above for placement, sew the circles in place by hand with a buttonhole stitch and 12-weight thread or two strands of embroidery floss. To add yo-yos to the flap, make yo-yos using a small yo-yo maker and charm squares.

Rosettes Pillow

Add dimensional detail to your couch or bed with this chic pillow.
Keep it muted or try bright rosettes for a dash of color.

✳ **FINISHED SIZE: 16" × 12"** ✳

MATERIALS

Yardage is based on 42"-wide fabric unless otherwise noted.

⅓ yard of white print for upper pillow and binding

¼ yard of cream print for lower pillow

5 strips, 2½" × 42", of assorted prints for rosettes
(I used 4 different prints.)

½ yard of muslin for lining (This will not show in
finished pillow.)

18" × 42" piece of lightweight cotton batting

12" × 16" pillow form

Optional: Turn-It-All turning tool for turning
fabric tubes

CUTTING

From the white print, cut:
1 strip, 6" × 42"
2 strips, 2¼" × 13"

From the cream print, cut:
1 strip, 8" × 42"

MAKING THE PILLOW COVER

Use a ¼"-wide seam allowance throughout,
unless otherwise noted.

1. Stitch the white 6" × 42" and cream 8" × 42"
strips together along the long edge and press.

2. Layer the muslin, the batting, and the pieced
rectangle (right side up). Quilt as desired by hand
or machine.

✳ **TERRY'S TIP**

Ideas for Quilting

Use a darning foot to meander or a
walking foot to quilt straight or wavy
lines. Anything goes—be creative!

allowances toward the resulting triangles. Repeat with the remaining two cream 3½" squares to make three.

Make 3.

3. In the same manner, sew a marked pink square to one end of *each* cream 2" × 3½" and 2" × 5" rectangle exactly as shown. **Pay attention to placement!** The marked lines must face in opposite directions exactly as shown.

Make 6.

Make 6.

4. Stitch a cream 2" square to each 2" × 5" unit as shown. Press the seam allowances toward the squares. Make six.

Make 6.

> ⁎ **TERRY'S TIP**
>
> ## Stitch Accurately
>
> An accurate ¼" seam allowance is very important for this runner!

5. Stitch the 2" × 3½" units from step 3 to opposite sides of the squares from step 2 as shown.

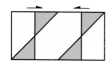

Make 3.

6. Stitch the units from step 4 to the top and bottom edges to complete the Little Sister Star blocks. Each block should measure 6½" square.

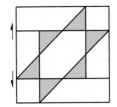

Make 3 blocks, 6½" square.

ASSEMBLING THE TABLE RUNNER

1. Mark a diagonal line on the wrong side of the 14 dark gray 3½" squares.

2. Position marked squares on opposite corners of each block exactly as shown. Stitch on the line. Trim the seam allowances to ¼". Press the seam allowances toward the resulting triangles.

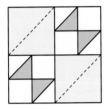 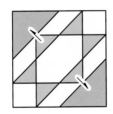

Make 3.

3. Position a marked square on one corner of a cream 6½" square. Stitch on the line. Trim the seam allowances to ¼" and press toward the triangle to make a setting square. Make eight. Set aside two cream 6½" squares.

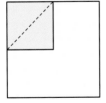 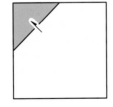

Make 8.

4. Arrange the three blocks in a diagonal row as shown above right. Place cream 6½" squares at each end. Fill in along the sides with the setting squares. Then add the cream triangles as shown.

5. Sew the pieces into rows. Press the seam allowances toward the setting squares. Join the rows to make the table runner. Press the seam allowances in the direction that makes the points look crisp.

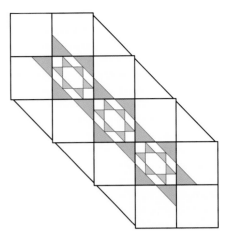

FINISHING THE TABLE RUNNER

You can download free finishing instructions at ShopMartingale.com/HowtoQuilt.

1. Fold the backing fabric in half, and then cut it in half at the fold. Sew the halves together end to end to make a 21" × 44" piece of backing.

2. Layer the table runner with batting and backing. Quilt as desired by hand or machine.

3. Trim the excess cream fabric by cutting exactly 3" from the dark-gray triangles as shown.

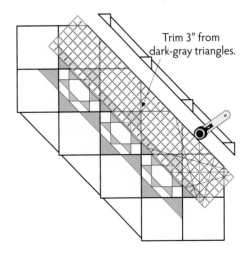

Trim 3" from dark-gray triangles.

4. Bind using the gray 2¼" x 42" strips.

Snowflake Table Runner

Get ready for the holidays quickly with this runner's quilt-as-you-go technique and easy raw-edge appliqué. After washing, the edges of the snowflakes fluff up for a cozy, wintry effect.

✳ FINISHED SIZE: 12½" × 40" ✳

Fine-point permanent marker
Magic Sizing or Mary Ellen's Best Press
Optional: 9½" × 9½" or larger square ruler
   for trimming short edges of runner

✳ TERRY'S TIP

Use the Right Supplies

I like to use Martingale's Papers for Foundation Piecing for stitching the appliqué. Lightweight copy paper will also work well. I trim the paper to 8½" × 8½" so that it's easy to center the snowflake on the paper.

MATERIALS

Yardage is based on 42"-wide fabric unless otherwise noted.

9 strips, 2½" × 42", of red and green prints
   (4 red and 5 green) for patchwork and binding
⅓ yard of white solid for snowflakes
½ yard of green print for backing
15" × 42" rectangle of batting
2 squares, 8½" x 8½", of foundation paper
   for appliqué

CUTTING

From the ½ yard of green print, cut:
1 rectangle, 15" × 42"

From the white solid, cut:
2 squares, 10" × 10"

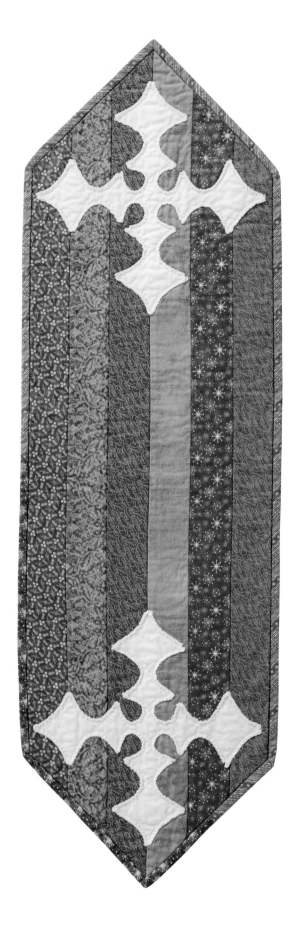

★ TERRY'S TIP

Rounding Down

The red and green strips should be about 40" to 42" long. It's OK if they're not all exactly the same length. The table runner can be trimmed in step 3 of "Making the Table Runner" to the length of the shortest strip.

MAKING THE TABLE RUNNER

Use a ¼"-wide seam allowance throughout, unless otherwise noted.

1. Center the batting on the wrong side of the green 15" × 42" rectangle. Pin a red or green 2½"-wide strip along the edge of the batting as shown, right side up. Using a walking foot, stitch a scant ¼" from the edge of the strip through all layers: the strip, the batting, and the backing.

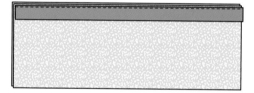

2. Pin the next red or green 2½"-wide strip on top of the first strip, with the edges even and right sides together. Using a walking foot, stitch a ¼" seam through all layers as shown. Fold the top strip over so the right side is facing up. Press.

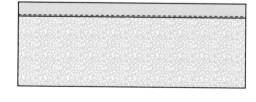

3. Continue adding strips in this manner across the panel until you've used six strips. Stitch along the raw edge of the last strip a scant ¼" from the edge. Trim the panel to 12½" × 40".

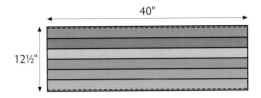

4. Mark and trim the ends as shown.

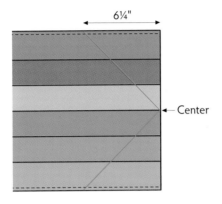

***

＊ TERRY'S TIP

Rulers to the Rescue

No need to measure if you have a square ruler—simply align opposite corners of the ruler along the center seam and trim.

***

APPLIQUÉING THE TABLE RUNNER

1. Using a fine-point permanent marker, trace two snowflakes onto 8½" squares of lightweight foundation paper using the pattern on page 63. (The markings from a ballpoint pen or pencil would rub off on the thread when you're stitching on the line, so a permanent marker works best.)

2. Press the white 10" squares using Mary Ellen's Best Press or Magic Sizing. Repeat several times until the squares are very crisp. This will keep them flat while you're stitching.

3. Position a starched white 10" square at each end of the runner as shown, *wrong side* facing the strippy side of the runner. The edges of the white square should be about 1" from the diagonal edges of the runner as shown. Pin.

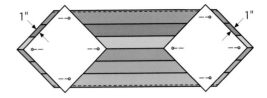

***

＊ TERRY'S TIP

Tips for Stitching Snowflakes

Place pins along the edges of the white square where you can easily pull them out while stitching. If you can see the strips through the white square, use a double layer of white for each snowflake.

***

4. Flip the runner to the wrong side and position a marked snowflake paper at each end of the runner as shown. The points of the snowflake should align with the centerline of stitching on the backing. The edge of the paper should be 1½" from the diagonal edges of the runner. Pin.

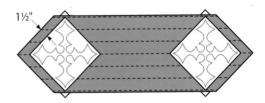

5. Stitch along the line on the paper, stitching through all layers. Use a small straight stitch (1.5 mm to 2 mm). Overlap stitches about ½" when you reach the starting point.

* *Clipping snowflake edges every ¼" results in beautifully raveled edges after laundering.*

* **TERRY'S TIP**

Appliqué Stitching Success

+ If you didn't use permanent ink, stitch just inside the line. The ink will tear away completely when you remove the paper.

+ For sharp points, stop with the needle down at the corner, lift the presser foot, and pivot. Lower the presser foot and continue stitching.

+ For smooth curves, stop with the needle down as needed, lift the presser foot, and adjust the fabric position. Lower the presser foot and continue stitching.

6. From the right side, trim just the white fabric layer a scant ¼" from the stitching. Be careful not to cut the runner by accident. Clip every ¼" to help the edges ravel. Tear the paper away on the back. Pull opposite corners of the fabric to loosen the paper.

FINISHING THE TABLE RUNNER

You can download free finishing instructions at ShopMartingale.com/HowtoQuilt.

1. Bind the runner using the remaining red and green 2½"-wide strips.

2. Wash the runner and dry in the dryer to fluff up the edges of the snowflakes.

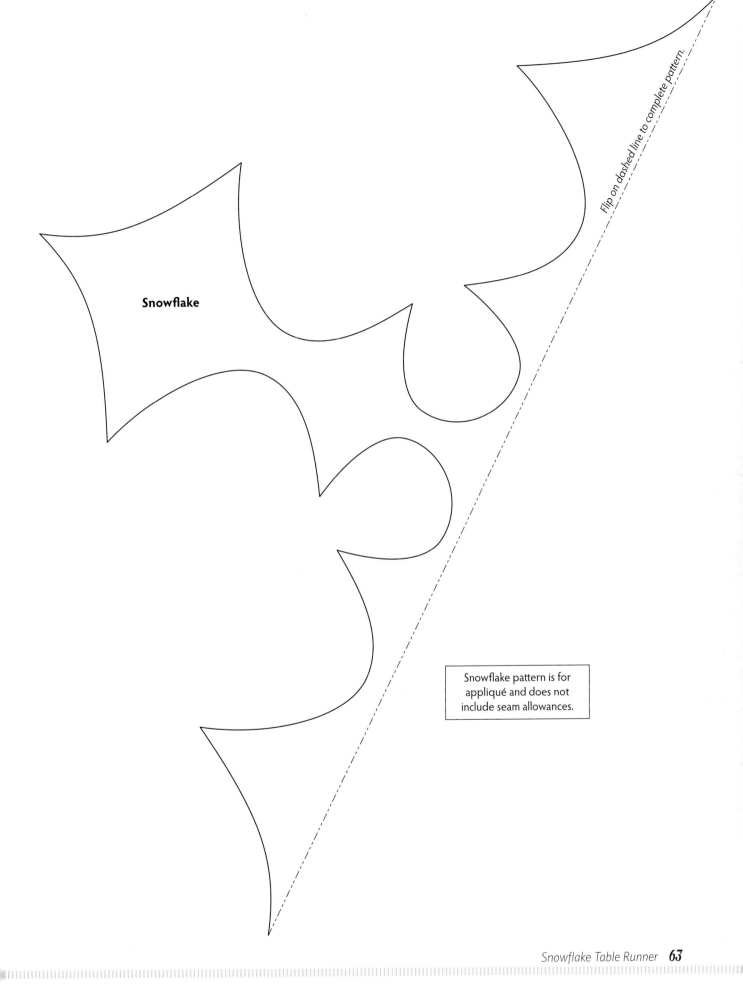

Snowflake

Flip on dashed line to complete pattern.

Snowflake pattern is for
appliqué and does not
include seam allowances.

Tic-Tac-Mo Table Runner

The squares in each block form a simple grid like the old-fashioned children's game. I made the center square larger because it's everyone's favorite. Tic-Tac-Mo was inspired by a tattered old quilt in a Missouri antique shop, and the Mo stands for Missouri.

✳ **FINISHED SIZE: 13⅜" × 36¾"** ✳

MATERIALS

Yardage is based on 42"-wide fabric unless otherwise noted. Fat quarters measure 18" × 21". Fat eighths measure 9" × 21".

⅝ yard of gray print for background and binding

1 fat quarter of white solid for blocks

3 fat eighths *OR* 3 squares, 10" × 10", of navy, teal, and coral prints for blocks

½ yard of backing fabric

18" × 41" rectangle of batting

Optional: 24"-long ruler for trimming long edges of runner

✳ **TERRY'S TIP**

Choosing Fabric

Choose a solid or an allover, non-directional print for the background.

CUTTING

From the gray print, cut;

1 strip, 7" × 42"; crosscut into:
    2 squares, 7" × 7"; cut each square into quarters diagonally to make 8 triangles
    4 rectangles, 4" × 7"
    4 rectangles, 2" × 7"

1 strip, 4" × 42"; crosscut into:
    1 strip, 4" × 20"
    1 strip, 4" × 10"
    2 squares, 3½" × 3½"

3 strips, 2¼" × 42"

From the white solid, cut:

2 strips, 2" × 20"

3 strips, 2" × 20"; crosscut into:
    1 strip, 2" × 10"
    12 rectangles, 2" × 4"

From *each* navy, teal, and coral print, cut:

1 square, 4" × 4" (3 total)

4 squares, 2" × 2" (12 total)

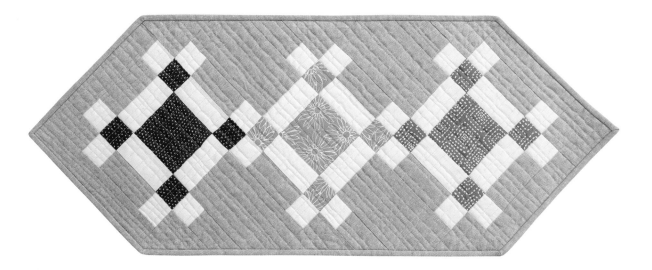

MAKING THE BLOCKS

Use a ¼"-wide seam allowance throughout.

1. Sew white 2" × 4" rectangles to opposite edges of each print 4" square. Press the seam allowances toward the print square. Each unit should measure 4" × 7".

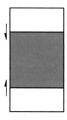

Make 3.

2. Sew matching print 2" squares to the ends of white 2" × 4" rectangles. Press the seam allowances toward the squares. The pieced rectangle should measure 2" × 7". Repeat to make two pieced rectangles from each print for a total of six pieced rectangles.

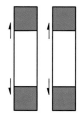

Make 2 from each print.

3. Matching the print used in the unit, sew the pieced rectangles to the long edges of a unit from step 1 to make a block. Press the seam allowances away from the center. The block should measure 7" square. Repeat to make one block from each print for a total of three blocks.

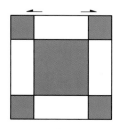

Make 3.

ASSEMBLING THE TABLE RUNNER

1. Sew the white 2" × 20" strips to the long edges of the gray 4" × 20" strip to make a strip set. Press the seam allowances toward the gray. The strip set should measure 7" × 20". Cut the strip set into eight 2"-wide A segments.

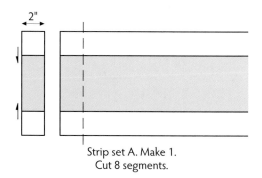

2"

Strip set A. Make 1.
Cut 8 segments.

2. Sew the white 2" × 10" strip to one long edge of the gray 4" × 10" strip to make a strip set. Press the seam allowances toward the gray. The strip set should measure 5½" × 10". Cut the strip set into four 2"-wide B segments.

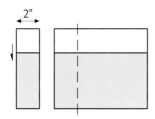

Strip set B. Make 1.
Cut 4 segments.

3. Sew a gray 2" × 7" rectangle to one A segment. Press the seam allowances toward the gray. The unit should measure 3½" × 7". Repeat to make four units. Set aside the remaining four A segments.

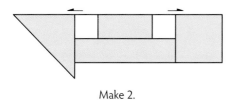

Make 4.

4. Position a unit from step 3 between a gray triangle and a gray 3½" square **exactly as shown.** Sew together. Press the seam allowances toward the gray. Repeat to make a second unit in the same manner. Set aside the remaining two units from step 3.

Make 2.

✶ TERRY'S TIP

Pay Attention!

The white squares should be at the top.

5. Position a gray triangle, a B segment, a gray 4" × 7" rectangle, and an A segment **exactly as shown.** Sew together. Press the seam allowances away from the white squares. Repeat to make four units total.

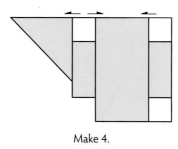

Make 4.

6. Arrange the blocks in a diagonal row as shown. Place the assorted units on the sides of the blocks exactly as shown. Position the units from step 4 on the top and bottom of the rows. Sew together the blocks and units in each row. Press the seam allowances toward the print blocks.

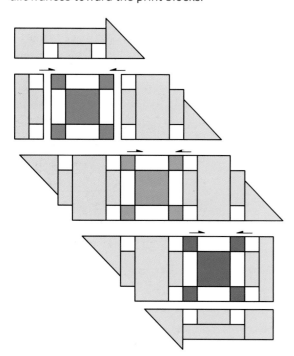

7. Sew the rows together to make the table-runner top. Press the seam allowances in one direction. Straighten the long edges of the runner with a rotary cutter as shown.

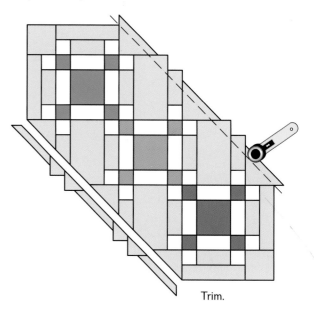

Trim.

FINISHING THE TABLE RUNNER

You can download free finishing instructions at ShopMartingale.com/HowtoQuilt.

1. Layer the table runner with batting and backing. Quilt as desired by hand or machine.

2. Bind using the gray 2¼"-wide strips.

Traveling Totes

Make these bags using your favorite fabric line. To make all five bags as a coordinated set, choose nine fat quarters and two different one-yard pieces. Show off the biggest print on the large bag and mix and match the rest of the fabrics in the other sizes.

FINISHED SIZES:

Mini tote: 3" × 7" × 2" (fits a water bottle)

Small tote: 5" × 9" × 2" (tote a travel iron or a ball of yarn and knitting needles)

Skinny tote: 3¾" × 12" × 3" (holds a curling iron or hair straightener)

Medium tote: 6¾" × 12½" × 3" (great for packing an iron or slippers)

Large tote: 13½" × 26½" × 6" (use as a laundry bag)

MATERIALS

Yardage is based on 42"-wide fabric unless otherwise noted. Fat quarters measure 18" × 21". Fat eighths measure 9" × 21".

Mini Tote, Small Tote, or Skinny Tote

1 fat quarter of main-color print for bag and casing
1 fat quarter of contrasting print for lining and ties

Medium Tote

1 fat quarter of main-color print for bag and casing
1 fat quarter of contrasting print A for lining
1 fat eighth of contrasting print B for ties

Large Tote

1 yard of main-color print for bag and casing
1 yard of contrasting print for lining and ties

CUTTING

Mini Tote

From the main-color print, cut:
1 strip, 8½" × 21"; crosscut into 1 rectangle, 8½" × 10½" (bag)
1 strip, 2½" × 21"; crosscut into 2 rectangles, 2½" × 5½" (casing)

From the contrasting print, cut:
1 strip, 8½" × 21"; crosscut into 1 rectangle, 8½" × 10½" (lining)
2 strips, 1½" × 21" (ties)

Continued on page 71

Continued from page 69

Small Tote

From the main-color print, cut:
1 strip, 10½" × 21"; crosscut into 1 rectangle,
   10½" × 14½" (bag)
1 strip, 2½" × 21"; crosscut into 2 rectangles,
   2½" × 7½" (casing)

From the contrasting print, cut:
1 strip, 10½" × 21"; crosscut into 1 rectangle,
   10½" × 14½" (lining)
2 strips, 1½" × 21" (ties)

Skinny Tote

From the main-color print, cut:
1 square, 14" × 14" (bag)
1 strip, 2½" × 21"; crosscut into 2 rectangles,
   2½" × 7¼" (casing)

From the contrasting print, cut:
1 square, 14" × 14" (lining)
2 strips, 1½" × 21" (ties)

Medium Tote

From the main-color print, cut:
1 rectangle, 14½" × 20" (bag)
1 strip, 2½" × 21"; crosscut into 2 rectangles,
   2½" × 10¼" (casing)

From contrasting print A, cut:
1 rectangle, 14½" × 20" (lining)

From contrasting print B, cut:
3 strips, 1½" × 21" (ties)

Large Tote

From the main-color print, cut:
1 rectangle, 30" × 40" (bag)
1 strip, 3" × 42"; crosscut into 2 rectangles,
   3" × 20¼" (casing)

From the contrasting print, cut:
1 rectangle, 30" × 40" (lining)
2 strips, 2" × 42" (ties)

⋆ **TERRY'S TIP**

Three More Options

For an insulated bag, layer the main-color print with cotton batting underneath. (Cut the batting the same size as the bag panel.) Quilt using a walking foot or darning foot. Because the quilted main-color rectangle may end up smaller, you may need to trim the lining to match.

For a speedy bag, skip the lining and finish your seams with zigzag stitching.

To make an over-the-shoulder strap for the mini tote, make one long tie using three strips.

MAKING THE TOTE

Use a ¼"-wide seam allowance throughout, unless otherwise noted. Follow these instructions for all sizes.

1. Fold under ¼" twice and stitch to hem each short end of the two casing rectangles. Press each rectangle in half lengthwise, wrong sides together.

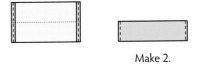

Make 2.

2. Fold the top edge of the bag rectangle (the longest edge of the rectangle) in half to find the center. Mark with a pin. With raw edges even, pin the casing rectangles ¼" from the center pin.

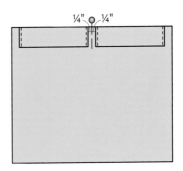

3. Sew the top edge of the lining rectangle to the top edge of the bag rectangle with the raw edges even and the casings in between. Press the seam allowance toward the main-color print.

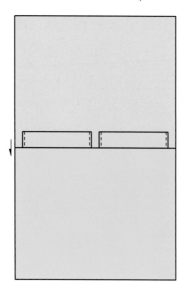

4. Fold the pieced rectangle in half lengthwise, right sides together and raw edges even. Pin the raw edges together at the casing seam. Stitch a ¼" seam along the raw edges, leaving a 3" opening at the center of the lining bottom. Pivot at the corners with the needle down. Backstitch at the beginning and end. For the larger bags you may want to leave a larger opening to make it easier to turn right side out.

Leave open 3".

5. With the tote still inside out, fold each corner as shown. Measure and mark a line for your size as shown. Stitch on the line. Trim the seam allowances to ¼". This will make the bottom of the tote flat. Stitch the corners on both the lining and the main-color print.

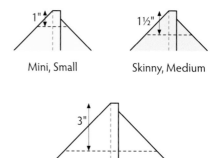

Mini, Small   Skinny, Medium

Large

6. Pull the bag through the opening in the lining to turn it right side out. Stitch the opening closed by hand or machine.

7. Tuck the lining inside the bag. Topstitch around the top of the bag through all layers, about ⅛" below the casing.

Topstitch.

MAKING THE TIES

1. Press the tie strips in half lengthwise, wrong sides together. Open and press both edges in to meet at the center crease. Refold the center crease and press again. Topstitch close to the edge. For the medium bag, stitch one and a half strips together for each tie.

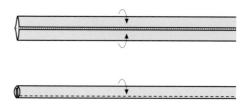

2. Thread one tie through both front and back casings, beginning and ending on the right-hand side. Knot the ends together. Thread the other tie through the opposite way, beginning and ending on the left-hand side. Knot the ends together. Trim the ends at an angle.

Wave Runner

This runner is a perfect fit for a table or chest of drawers that's positioned against a wall. It's great for a buffet meal—there's plenty of room to arrange serving dishes or beverages without covering up the pretty edge. One version has a decorative sashing strip and a scallop edge, while the other has a wave edge and yo-yos for extra flair.

FINISHED SIZES:

Scallop-edge runner (at right):
14½" × 37"

Wave-edge runner (page 78):
13½" × 41½"

MATERIALS

Yardage is based on 42"-wide fabric unless otherwise noted. Makes 1 runner with either a wave or scallop edge.

⅜ yard of multicolored floral for table-runner top
¼ yard of cream print for wave or scallop border
½ yard of red print for sashing strip and binding
⅝ yard of backing fabric
19" × 44" rectangle of batting
Water-soluble marker
Freezer paper for cutting template
Optional:

* ⅛ yard of fabric for yo-yos

* Scallop Radial Rule (Katie Lane Quilts) for marking scallops

* Large 45 mm (orange) Yo-Yo Maker (Clover)

CUTTING

All strips are cut on the straight grain unless otherwise noted.

From the multicolored floral, cut:
1 strip, 10½" × 42"

From the cream print, cut:
1 strip, 4½" × 42"

Continued on page 76

* TERRY'S TIP

Using a Yo-Yo Maker

If you're using the Clover Yo-Yo Maker, follow these steps to make the yo-yos.

1. Center the disc on the wrong side of a 4¼" fabric square. Pop the fabric and disc into the tray, aligning a ridge on the disc with a bump on the edge of the tray. Trim the fabric corners. Knot a length of quilting thread. Stitch in and out of each crescent-shaped hole. I like to hold the yo-yo maker with the disc facing away from me and use my fingers underneath to hold the seam allowance under as I stitch.

2. When you've stitched all the way around the disc, pop the disc out by pushing your finger through the hole in the tray. Take the disc out of the yo-yo. Pull both ends of the thread to gather the edges toward the center. Adjust the gathers as you pull, wiggling the edges to make the yo-yo nice and flat.

3. Pull the threads tight and knot the ends together several times. I like to pull the threads through to the back of the yo-yo and take a few teeny backstitches to anchor the threads.

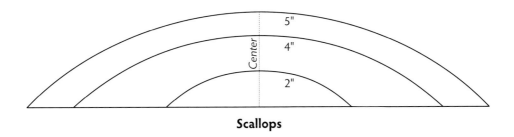

Scallops

Wine Zip

Bring the best-dressed wine bottle to any party. Zip up two coordinating fabrics with a contrasting zipper and you'll be celebrating in style.

✳ **FINISHED SIZE: Fits a standard wine bottle** ✳

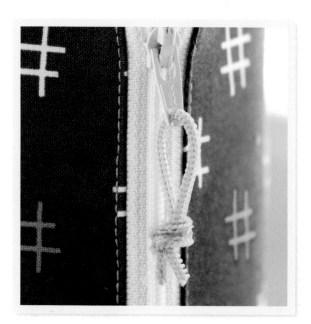

MATERIALS

Fat quarters measure 18" × 21".

1 fat quarter of navy print for exterior
1 fat quarter of green print for lining and binding
½ yard of 20"-wide woven fusible interfacing, such as Pellon SF101
14"-long coil zipper*
Zipper foot
Freezer paper for cutting template

*A 22"-long coil zipper may be used instead, giving you enough length to make a matching zipper pull using the extra length of zipper coil.

Optional:

✳ Wonder Clips (Clover) for securing multiple layers of fabric
✳ Curved Corner Cutter (Creative Grids) for rounding curves
✳ Clear-drying glue for decorative zipper pull

CUTTING

From the navy print, cut:
1 rectangle, 10½" × 16"

From the green print, cut:
1 rectangle, 10½" × 16"
1 strip, 2¼" × 12"

From the fusible interfacing, cut:
2 rectangles, 10" × 15½"

MAKING THE ZIP

Use a ¼"-wide seam allowance throughout unless otherwise noted.

1. Following the manufacturer's instructions, center and fuse an interfacing 10" × 15½" rectangle to the wrong sides of the navy and the green 10½" × 16" rectangles.

2. Measure and mark lines exactly as shown on page 82 onto the **right side** of the green rectangle along one 10½" edge (this will be the bottom of the wine zip). Trace the bottom-curve pattern (page 84) onto freezer paper and cut out on the drawn lines to make a template. Use the template to mark the curves as shown. (The Curved Corner

Cutter may also be used to mark the curves; use the 1½" radius curve.) Use scissors to cut the straight lines as shown. **Do NOT** cut the curves yet! Repeat with the navy rectangle.

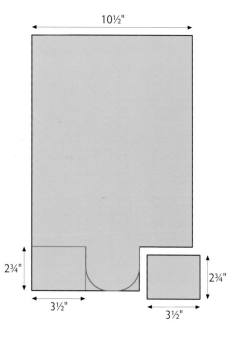

★ TERRY'S TIP

Cut in Half the Time

To save time, stack the navy and green prints and cut them both at once!

3. Pin the zipper to the long edge of the navy rectangle, right sides together. Align the top edge of the zipper tape with the raw edge of the fabric. The zipper pull should face down! Stitch a scant ¼" from the edge. Layer the green rectangle on top, wrong side up, with the edges even. Stitch a ¼" seam as shown through all the layers.

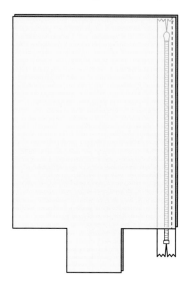

★ TERRY'S TIP

Clip Instead of Pin

For easier stitching, I use Wonder Clips rather than pins. They're quick to remove and have no sharp points. Then, to reduce bulk near your machine needle, unzip the zipper before beginning to sew.

4. Fold the navy and green rectangles away from the zipper. Topstitch about ⅛" from the fold, stitching through all layers.

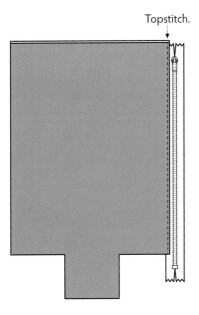

Topstitch.

5. Fold the navy layer in half lengthwise, right sides together and the raw edge even with the edge of the zipper tape. Pin. Stitch a scant ¼" seam.

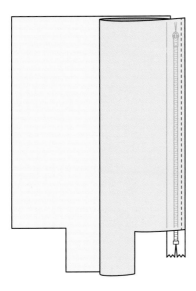

6. Fold the green layer in half lengthwise, right sides together and the raw edge even with the zipper tape. Stitch through all layers.

7. Turn the wine zip right side out. Unzip the zipper. Finger-press the navy and green prints away from the zipper. Topstitch about ⅛" from the fold, stitching through all layers.

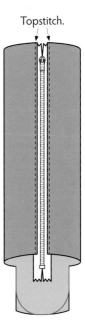

Topstitch.

8. Close the zipper to prepare for sewing across the coil. Stitch along the bottom edge through both layers, stitching a scant ¼" from the raw edge and a scant ¼" inside the marked curves.

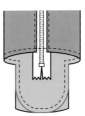

9. Cut along the marked curves. Trim the bottom end of the zipper even with the fabric. Clip the straight edge about every ½", just up to the stitching. Do not clip through the stitching.

10. Turn the bag inside out. Mark the center of the curved edge. Matching the marked center to the zipper teeth, pin and stitch the bottom seam. The clips will spread open to help the edge fit along the curve. Backstitch at the beginning and end of the seam. Zigzag the seam allowance to prevent raveling.

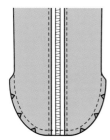

FINISHING

You can download free binding instructions at ShopMartingale.com/HowtoQuilt.

1. Unzip the zipper. Press the green 2¼" × 12" strip in half lengthwise with wrong sides together.

2. Leaving at least ½" of binding extending beyond the zipper, stitch the binding to the top edge of the wine zip. Press the binding strip toward the top raw edge of the wine zip, and then trim the binding ends ½" from the zipper edge. Wrap the ends to the back to cover the edge, and then fold the binding to the back. Stitch in place by hand or machine.

✳ **TERRY'S TIP**

Decorative Zipper Pull

For a snazzy zipper pull, try a piece of a matching or contrasting zipper. Unzip and use just one side of the zipper. You'll need about 5".

Using sharp scissors, trim right next to the zipper coil (what would be called the "teeth" on a metal zipper). Pull any loose threads away from the coil. Thread the trimmed coil through the zipper pull and tie the ends in an overhand knot. Trim the ends. Put a dot of clear-drying glue on the knot if desired.

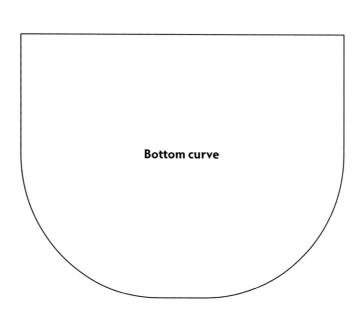

Bottom curve

Zipper-Pocket Gift Wrap

For kids of any age, wrap a two-liter drink bottle and tuck pizza or movie coupons into the zipper pocket. Coffee lovers will enjoy a coffee gift card zipped up around a thermos. For someone on the go, stash some cash in the pocket and wrap around a water bottle. One size fits all!

✳ **FINISHED SIZE: 4¾" × 15¾"** ✳

MATERIALS

Fat quarters measure 18" × 21". Fat eighths measure 9" × 21". Charm squares measure 5" × 5".

1 fat quarter of gray print for backing and tie
8 charm squares or 4 fat eighths of assorted prints (green, gray, and aqua) for front
¼ yard of 22"-wide fusible fleece, such as Pellon 987FP
14"-long coil zipper (it will be trimmed to size)
Zipper foot
Optional: Mary Ellen's Best Press

CUTTING

From the gray print, cut:
2 strips, 1¾" × 21"
2 rectangles, 6" × 17"

If using charm squares of assorted prints, set aside 2 squares; then from the remaining prints, cut:
16 strips, 1½" × 5"

If using fat eighths of assorted prints, cut:
2 squares, 5" × 5"
16 strips, 1½" × 5"

From the fusible fleece, cut:
1 rectangle, 5" × 16¾"

MAKING THE WRAP

Use a ¼"-wide seam allowance throughout, unless otherwise noted.

1. To prepare the lining, center and fuse the fleece 5" × 16¾" rectangle to the wrong side of one gray 6" × 17" rectangle, following the manufacturer's instructions.

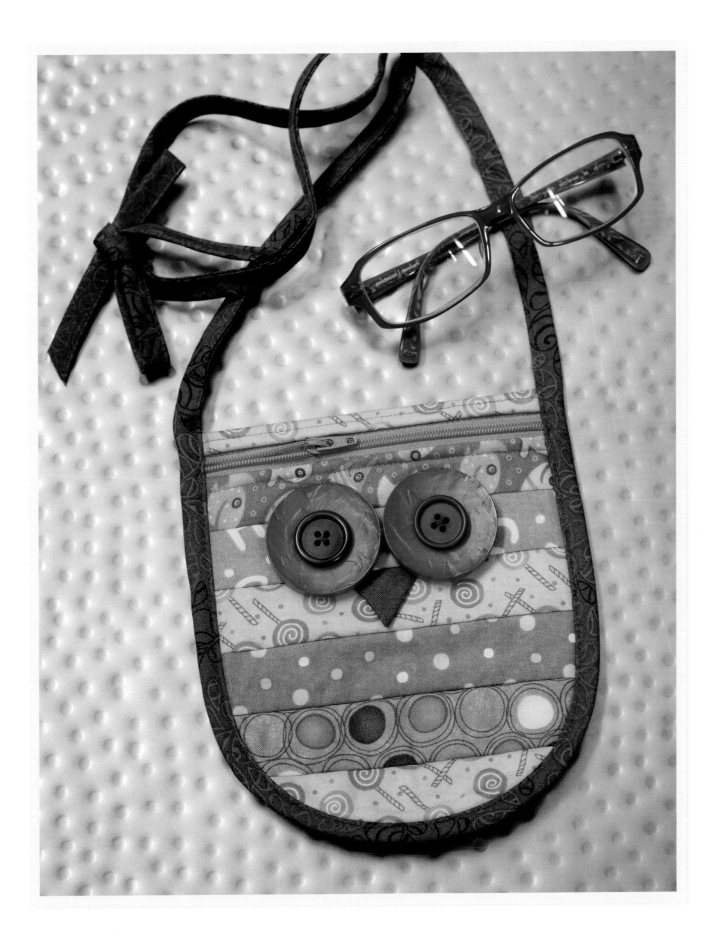

2. Place the first two assorted strips with right sides together along the fleece side of a brown rectangle as shown. Stitch through all layers: the strips, the fleece, and the brown print. Fold the top strip over so the right side is facing up and finger-press the seam.

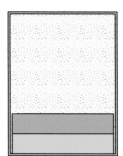

✳ **TERRY'S TIP**

Walking Foot

Use a walking foot so the layers don't shift while sewing. Move the needle position as needed to get an accurate ¼" seam. Set the stitch length to 2.5 mm to 3 mm.

3. Continue adding strips in this manner, working across the panel as shown until you've added eight strips. Stitch across the top strip, close to the raw edge, and trim the excess fleece and lining. This is the back panel.

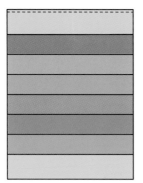

4. To make the beak, fold the brown 3" square in half, wrong sides together, and press. Fold it in thirds as shown and press again. Trim across the top edge to straighten the edge.

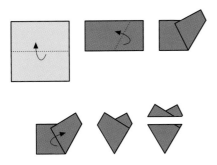

5. To make the front panel, stitch four assorted strips to the fleece side of the remaining brown rectangle in the same manner as for the back panel. Center the beak on the fourth strip with the top raw edges even; pin in place. Add two more assorted strips, securing the beak. Stitch across the edge of the top strip close to the raw edge; trim the excess fleece and lining.

6. Center the zipper on the top edge of the front panel with right sides together and the zipper pull facing down. Stitch a ¼" seam through all the layers. Finish the seam with a zigzag or decorative stitch to prevent raveling.

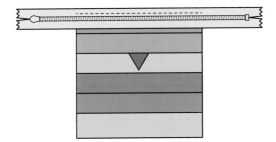

7. Fold the front panel away from the zipper and topstitch a scant ¼" from the fold, making sure to catch the edge of the zipper tape underneath.

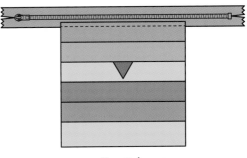

Topstitch.

8. Repeat steps 6 and 7 on the other half of the zipper using the back panel. Stack the buttons as shown and stitch them next to the beak.

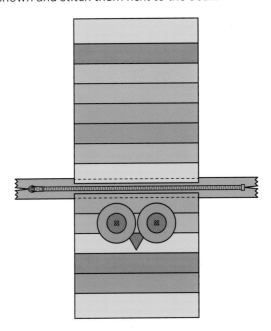

9. Wrap the back of the bag around the top half of the zipper, aligning the edges of the back and front panels. Stitch again on the previous stitching line through all layers.

10. Trace the pattern on page 95 onto freezer paper and cut out. Position the paper template at the bottom edge of the bag and trace around the curve. Move the zipper pull to the center and stitch close to the edge along the sides and bottom of the bag as shown. Trim the zipper and curved edge next to the stitching.

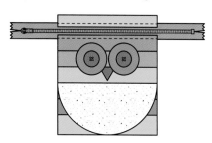

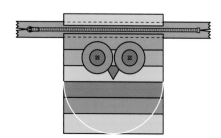

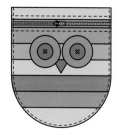

Trim.

FINISHING THE ZIP

1. Stitch the brown 2½"-wide strips together with a diagonal seam. Press in half lengthwise, wrong sides together. Mark the center of the long binding strip with a pin.

2. Match the center of the binding strip to the center of the bag bottom. With raw edges even, stitch the binding along the side and bottom edges of the bag. Fold the binding around to the back and press. Fold the long binding ends in thirds with the raw edges tucked in. Stitch along the edge of the binding, close to the folded edge, catching all of the layers as you stitch.

3. Tie the ends together for the desired strap length and trim the ends at an angle.

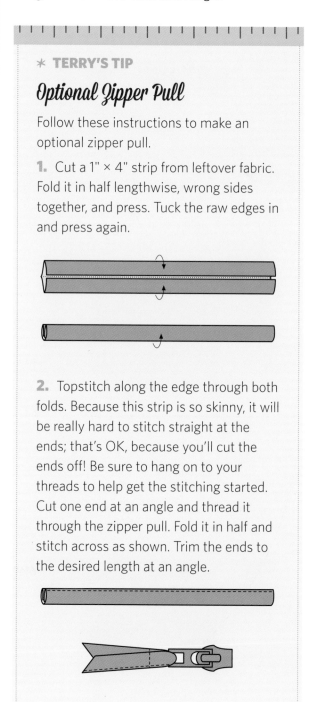

★ **TERRY'S TIP**

Optional Zipper Pull

Follow these instructions to make an optional zipper pull.

1. Cut a 1" × 4" strip from leftover fabric. Fold it in half lengthwise, wrong sides together, and press. Tuck the raw edges in and press again.

2. Topstitch along the edge through both folds. Because this strip is so skinny, it will be really hard to stitch straight at the ends; that's OK, because you'll cut the ends off! Be sure to hang on to your threads to help get the stitching started. Cut one end at an angle and thread it through the zipper pull. Fold it in half and stitch across as shown. Trim the ends to the desired length at an angle.

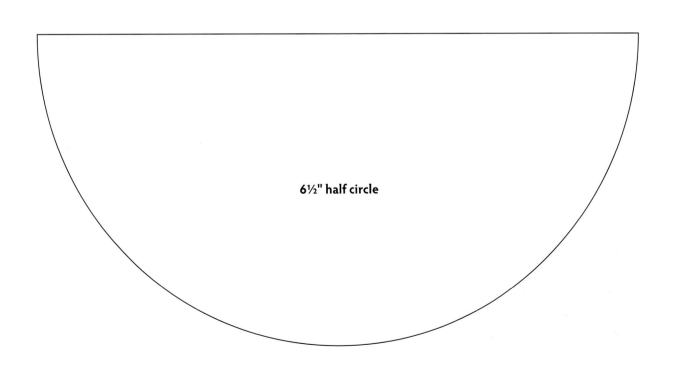

6½" half circle

Acknowledgments

Many thanks to my husband, Kirk, who runs the business end of things at Atkinson Designs, and to my wonderful assistant, Greta Anderson, who is always ready to dive in and help wherever she is needed.

About the Author

TERRY ATKINSON lives in Elk River, Minnesota, and has been designing sewing and quilting patterns for over 20 years. When she's not getting creative and playing with fabric in her sewing room, you can find her exploring the great outdoors in her retro Shasta camper.

Watch "Terry's Tips" how-to videos at her website: AtkinsonDesigns.com